The Face of Grace

*Knowing & Living
True Grace*

The Face of Grace

*Knowing & Living
True Grace*

Wade Burleson

The Face of Grace: Knowing & Living True Grace
Copyright © 2020 by Wade Burleson

All rights reserved. No part of this publication may be reproduced, stored in a retrieval system, or transmitted in any form or by any means—electronic, mechanical, photocopy, recording, or any other—except for brief quotations in printed reviews, without the prior permission of the publisher.

Printed in the United States of America. First Printing, 2020

Scripture quotations taken from the New American Standard Bible® NASB, Copyright © 1960, 1962, 1963, 1968, 1971, 1972, 1973, 1975, 1977, 1995 by The Lockman Foundation. Used by permission. www.Lockman.org

Istoria Ministries
1112 W. York, Enid, Oklahoma, 73703
istoriaministries@gmail.com

MCGAHAN PUBLISHING HOUSE
Tullahoma, Tennessee 37388, U.S.A.
www.mphbooks.com
Requests for information should be sent to:
info@mphbooks.com

Cover Design by Taylor Blasier

ISBN 978-1-951252-09-0 (paperback)

Acknowledgments

The Face of Grace is the composite work of many people. First and foremost, I would like to thank my mother, Mary Burleson, a professional editor during her career, for her tireless and indefatigable transcription and proofing of a series of messages I taught entitled *The Face of Grace*. Without her, this book would not be in your hands.

I would also like to thank a team around Mary Burleson, including Fred Cherry and Jenny McMonigle, my mom's brother and sister respectively, for their proofreading and suggestions. In addition, Paul Burleson, my father, a writer and theologian par excellence, for his critical eye.

Lissa Roberson, a former missionary to China, worked hard to edit content and create group discussion questions. Rachelle and I had the privilege of visiting Lissa and her husband Stu on the mission field in China before they retired, and we are grateful for their friendship.

Speaking of Rachelle (my wife), I am always grateful for her support and encouragement. I may write about grace, but she lives it! Thank you, Rachelle!

Finally, the people of Emmanuel Enid have been those I've served for the last three decades. They've been my friends, my extended family, and my greatest supporters. They were the ones who originally listened to these messages as I spoke them during a

Sunday morning series. I have stayed at Emmanuel Enid for as long as I have because I do not believe there exists a greater group of people in America than those I know at Emmanuel Enid.

The spoken word is not like the written word. Please forgive any idioms or expressions that don't translate well in print. We've taken what was in my heart and put it on paper. All errors are mine alone, and I trust God will use even my mistakes for His glory and your good.

I trust after reading The Face of Grace you will truly be able to identify grace when you see it, experience it, or give it.

In Christ's Eternal Grace,

Wade Burleson
October 20, 2020

Contents

Acknowledgments   5
Foreword   9

SECTION I: A MIND THAT THINKS   15
Chapter 1: Never Worthy; Always Loved   17
Chapter 2: Never Desiring; Always Chosen   27
Chapter 3: Never Perfect; Always Embraced   41
Chapter 4: Never Seeking; Always Pursued   53
Chapter 5: Never Finishing; Always Completed   67

SECTION II: A MOUTH THAT SPEAKS   77
Chapter 6: Talks *To* People, Not *About* People   79
Chapter 7: Speaks Intentionally, Not Rashly   93
Chapter 8: Builds, Not Destroys   107
Chapter 9: Speaks Gently, Not Harshly   119
Chapter 10: Speaks for Others' Good, Not My Gain   133

SECTION III: EYES THAT SEE   145
Chapter 11: See the Best in People   147
Chapter 12: Cover the Sins of People   157
Chapter 13: Avoid the Craving for People   169
Chapter 14: Focus on the Needs of People   181
Chapter 15: Are Open to the Frailty of People   191

SECTION IV: EARS THAT HEAR 203
Chapter 16: Hear the Word of Christ 205
Chapter 17: Are Deaf to the Lies of this World 219
Chapter 18: Are Sensitive to the Hurts of People 233
Chapter 19: Really Hear the Truth of Your Identity 245
Chapter 20: Discern the Fire of God: Grace vs. Judgment 257

FINAL CHALLENGE 271

Foreword

This book is about GRACE.

Grace has been the theme of my life and ministry since I memorized the entire book of Romans as a boy (King James Version, no less!). I became captivated by the Apostle Paul's description of God's favor for His people, and the promises that God made to us that have nothing to do with our performance or success at being the kind of Christian we want to be.

I began to understand that grace is different than what most of us hear or experience in Sunday School or church. It led me down a path of trying to discover not only what God's grace looks like in my life, but also questioning what grace—real grace—looks like in my relationship with other people.

In other words, I began wondering about *The Face of Grace.*

There are a growing number of Americans who have either a phone or a computer with facial recognition capabilities. I am one of those Americans. I own a computer with facial recognition technology. This means that I can look at the camera lens on the front screen of the computer, and an internal facial recognition software program takes key measurements of my face. Once that image is saved, my face is recognized within my computer system and powerup will take me to my home screen automatically without my touching a key.

Facial recognition is secure and simple to use because each human face is unique, and the scientific measurements of the face are as unique as a person's thumbprint or fingerprint. It is also a technology that is spreading throughout the world. You can't go to a major airport in the United States and enter its terminal these days without having your face scanned by the airport's security computer system. Churches, schools, malls, and other "soft targets" for terrorists are all considering implementing facial recognition technology for security purposes. You might think, "Wow, that's so uncomfortably 'Big Brother.'"

It might surprise you even more to know that some department stores are using facial recognition technology for purposes other than security. There's a major retail chain in Oklahoma where every time you walk in the door, the store's computer system scans your face with facial recognition software. An additional software program tracks the items you pull off the shelves to examine, then details the items you purchase afterward.

This store chain recently got into big trouble because their marketing department had begun sending baby product coupons to young women who didn't even know they were pregnant yet! You might be wondering how the marketing department knew which young women to target with their mother-to-be advertising campaign. It knew by the women's shopping patterns based upon facial recognition technology, by store cameras that watched shoppers browse the shelves, and the sales receipts that itemized their purchases. They knew that these young women were most likely on the verge of being with child because the stores had tracked their shopping patterns for months. They also knew it was very likely, based upon their research of products

Foreword

women examined on the shelves and ultimately purchased, that the young women would soon be pregnant. Now that is Big Brother-worthy! My point is that much can be known about a person by scanning a face for recognition and then watching that person's unique habits. We had better get used to facial recognition technology because it is here to stay.

Your face is like no other face in the world. Period. Just like there's not one snowflake that falls from the sky that is duplicated or replicated in the form or shape of another snowflake, neither is your face replicated in another. Now, I'm not calling you, me, or anybody else a snowflake. I'm only emphasizing that your face is eternally unique. Even those blessed with an identical twin carry unique measurements of the face that are different even from their twin! I think you now understand the power of facial recognition, so I'd like to ask you a question.

What is the "facial recognition" of grace? What does grace look like? How can you recognize God's grace, and how do you know if you are showing grace to others? What are the unique features of true grace? You might say that you're a Christian saved by grace. You may even talk about God's grace (or sing about it). But what are we talking about when we speak of grace?

As I write this, my friend Abraham Wright and his wife Marge are about to have a baby. They know through modern technology that the baby in Marge's womb will be a boy. Pastor Abraham and Marge are naming him Isaac. I've seen a sonogram picture of the baby, and Isaac's face resembles Abraham's face. His nose, his eyes, his cheek bones, all resemble his dad's. Isaac isn't identical to his dad, but you sure can tell Isaac bears the image of his father.

When God gave you His grace, (the Bible calls it "being born again"), you received the Spirit of God in your soul. He's "the God of all grace" (I Peter 5:10) and He made you part of His family. The God of all grace brings to life His kids who end up resembling Him. But what does GRACE look like? I can lie and tell somebody that I'm related to someone when I'm not, and I might even be able to convince you that my lie is true. But if I put my face in front of a computer, science and technology will tell the truth of who I am. In similar fashion, someone may lie and tell others they are a "child of God," or "a Christian," but when you understand the face of grace, you'll be able to tell whether or not the truth is being spoken.

So, again, what is the "face of grace"? It's easier for someone to describe grace than it is to define it. It's a little bit like if someone requested me regarding my wife Rachelle, "Wade, define Rachelle for me." I would be hard-pressed to give you an accurate *definition*, but I can describe my wife beautifully for you. If you pressed a person who believes in God to define grace, you might get the following definition: grace is unmerited favor, or kindness undeserved. But grace can be so much more beautifully *described* than it can be *defined*.

As you begin reading this book, I want you to know that it is my desire to convince you of a principle that will help you live your life to the fullest. Until you are captivated by God's amazing grace for you, you'll never be able to show, give, or convey grace to others. I write this book to help you become captivated by God's grace, which will empower you to be a person of grace in relation to others.

Do you understand that God's kindness to you is undeserved? Do you comprehend that the Creator's favor shown to you is undeserved? Do you know that grace can only be given to the unworthy? If someone deserves it, then it ceases to be grace and becomes something merited, deserved, or earned. When you work, you perform, and you are paid wages for your performance. Grace is the opposite of wages. If its grace, you don't work for it. If it's work, you're paid something for your performance. If it's grace, it's a gift—undeserved.

God shows grace to us even though we are unworthy of His favor. Do you grasp the significance of this statement? If you grew up in a religious setting, the teaching you received may well be dissimilar to what you'll be reading in this book. If you come from a background of institutional religion, you've probably been trained to think that God is kind toward you and shows favor to you because you do something, because you change something, or because you promise something.

Those "somethings" vary from religion to religion, but the religious principle is the same no matter the institution. Once you *do* something, then God will suddenly say, "Okay, there you go, now you're worthy! Now I will love you and I will be kind to you."

That's not the Face of Grace. That's not what God's grace looks like. That's not an image of God's kindness. That's not a description of His mercy. God is gracious to us though we'll never be worthy. God is kind to us though we'll never measure up. And until we are captivated by that, we will never convey grace to other people.

I have a book that I have loved since I was a kid. It is *Great Expectations* written by Charles Dickens. I love anything that Dickens authored because he was such a visual writer. A visual writer is one who can write a sentence, allowing the reader to almost magically develop an image in his mind while he reads. That's the gift of visual writing. As an example, this is how Charles Dickens described John Wemmick, a main character in *Great Expectations*. "John Wemmick has a 'post-office mouth' used for 'sorting and relating information.'" That was Dickens' vivid way of describing Wemmick's tendency to gossip.

I want to be like Dickens in this book, and visually describe through my writing how a graced person talks, what a graced person hears, and why a graced person sees life differently than those without grace. I would like to thank several people for their contributions in making this book possible.

My mother, a professional editor, took the audio recordings of a series of messages I gave to the church where I serve, and she transcribed the words to paper. My father, Paul Burleson, a longtime and well-known pastor, read through the manuscript my mother gave him for content suggestions. Fred Cherry and Jenny McMonigle, my maternal aunt and uncle, read through each chapter for editorial suggestions, and ultimately my professional editor mother sent me a complete transcript. Lissa Roberson, a long-time missionary and skilled editor herself, followed up with her professional eye for stylistic purposes. Each of these individuals has played a vital role in getting this book into your hands.

Finally, I would like to thank my wife, Dr. Rachelle Burleson, who has been a tremendous encouragement to me throughout our marriage. Our home is like a laboratory to put into practice what we believe about God and His grace, and I can't think of a better partner in putting into practice what we believe about God.

May God use this book to help us all recognize and reflect on *The Face of Grace*.

Section I

A Mind That Thinks

Chapter One

"Never Worthy; Always Loved"

Luke 6:27–36
"To you who are listening I say: Love your enemies…"

Until you and I are captivated by God's grace for us, we will never be able to convey God's grace to others. Until we understand that God loved us when we saw Him as our enemy, we'll never be able to love those who consider us their enemy. We must ask ourselves, "Are we truly aware that God's kindness to us is undeserved? Do we comprehend that the favor our Creator is pouring out on us comes when we least deserve it?" Do we understand and grasp what grace looks like?

God is gracious to us and we will never be worthy. He is kind to us and we will never measure up. Until we are captivated by this, until this truth brings joy to our souls, we will never make God's grace evident to other people. Let's look at three very important verses in Scripture to build and develop the theme of the Face of Grace.

The Apostle Paul said, God speaking: "My grace is sufficient for you" (II Corinthians 12:9). This is how Paul said he regarded his life: he understood that it was God's grace that was sufficient for him. Remember that Paul had been beaten. He had been thrown into prison. He went through a period where he was starving. Everybody turned against him, but God taught him, "My grace, Paul, is sufficient for you." Do we understand that? Do we believe it? What does this mean for us?

Part of my job is basically to attend to people when their world shatters. I get calls, emails, sometimes six or seven office visits a week from people who have hit rock bottom. A spouse has walked out. A divorce is pending. A job has been lost. A child has been arrested, or worse, suffered an auto accident, a rollover running from police. I talk to people who have themselves been arrested for drug possession. It's amazing how this world that we are living in is a world so full of hurt. During these conversations when I'm with these people at their lowest, I wish I could convince them of the significance and impact of the phrase, "My grace is sufficient for you."

I would say to them, "You see, it's not our job that is sufficient. It's not even our spouse who is sufficient for us. It's not our kids. It's not our reputation. All of those kinds of things are important, but they come and go. It's His benevolence toward us as unworthy persons that makes life sufficient."

"By His grace, I am who I am" (I Cor. 15:10). If you were to ask the average male, "Who are you?" most would state their name and what it is they do. "I am Wade Burleson. I am Pastor of Emmanuel Enid." That's not who I am. That's what I do. Most men get their identity from what they do. That's why when a man loses his job it's a very depressing time. If you ask a woman, most but not all will respond with words that describe relationships like wife or mother, those to whom she is related. These all are fine answers, but this is not who we are.

I am who I am by the grace of God. In other words, in our lowest points of life, we discover what Paul meant when he said God's grace was sufficient for him. When we understand the sufficiency of being loved and favored by God in our unworthiness, when we don't deserve it, His love and favor is sufficient for us and gives us our identity.

"Walk consistent with your calling" (Eph. 4:1). When we are captivated by the truth that our God calls us to Himself by pure grace, then we can live in our relationship to others "consistent with our calling of grace."

You see, the theme of Scripture is quite clear. God in His kindness toward undeserving sinners like us, reached out in grace and bestowed favor on the unworthy. He chased us down in His love and He transformed us by the power of His love. When we've been captivated by His grace, we will live a life consistent with our calling of grace.

What that means is this: people of grace should live gracious lives. Do we really comprehend the grace of God for us? Does it register to us that we are not worthy?

Sad to say, it does not register with most church-going people that they are "not" worthy. Most church people think they are worthy. That's one of the reasons why God in His love for us will often pull the rug out from under us, because our loving Heavenly Father would rather have us on our backs looking up to Him and His love for unworthy people, than He would for His people to stand upright and think we deserve what He did. The Bible teaches us that pride comes before a fall. "Pride goes before destruction, and a haughty spirit before a fall" (Prov. 16:18).

So I want to ask you again, do we comprehend, and are we captivated by God's grace for us? If so, then we can't help but be gracious toward the people around us. But why do we have churches full of Christians who don't live graciously? What's the reason? I would say it's because we have a lot of preachers who never draw their people to a place where they are captivated with the grace of God. Instead, most preachers focus their listeners' attention on what they "should be doing", or how we (the body) can perform to receive God's favor. Nothing about a works- oriented message inspires a believer to go out in the world and live out benevolence, kindness and mercy.

It reminds me of a little boy named Johnny who was going home from church one Sunday. He was in the back seat and Mom and Dad were in the front, and for some reason this normally talkative boy was unusually quiet. Mom and Dad kept turning around and asking, are you okay? Are you okay? Finally, Johnny spoke and said, "The preacher said today that he wanted all of us to grow up in Christian homes, but I want to stay with you guys."

We can say we are Christian, but it's the face of grace that proves it. Let's look now at a description of the **mind** of grace. A person of grace has:

A mind that thinks,
Never Worthy; Always Loved

Do we think like that?

By the way, before we go any further, let me just give a caveat here. We are referring to relationships. We are referring to our relationship with God and our relationship with others. We are not referring to work. Work is a contract of employment that is based upon merit and performance. That is why you are paid wages. You cannot go to your boss tomorrow and say to him, "Listen boss, I didn't do what you told me to do, and I know I haven't performed in my job, but Pastor Wade said that we are to be people of grace, so go ahead and pay me what I don't deserve. After all, that's grace." He will fire you so fast your head will spin. And you know what? He should, because your work is not a contract of grace. No. No. No. It's a contract of performance.

Here's a second caveat that's going to rock your world. Most people treat their marriages as an employment contract, which is not the way it's supposed to be. When God established the institution of marriage, it was to be a beautiful picture of God's relationship with us. The marriage covenant is to model the love of God for His people. That's why any time the writers of the New Testament address husbands and encourage them to act a certain way toward their wives, what do they say? "Husbands love your wives even as Christ has loved you." We are encouraged to model and mirror Christ's love for us in the love we have for our spouse.

Now the problem is we get all confused about how Christ has loved us because we don't understand the principles of grace. Because of this, we mistakenly change our marriage covenant into an employment contract based on performance, rather than a relationship patterned after grace.

The one loved (in a relationship of grace) is never good enough, but real love never requires it. This is how God is gracious to us. God loves us and we will never be worthy. Again, any time we get into this mindset of being worthy of the favor of God, we are in trouble because what happens is we perceive God a certain way, and then all we do is project that to other people. God is gracious to us and we are not worthy. He loves us and we never measure up.

"If you love those who love you…do not even the tax gatherers do the same? And if you greet your brothers only, what do you do more than others? Do not even the Gentiles do the same" (Matthew 5:47–48)?

The phrase "tax gatherers" is the Biblical way of describing lost people, people who do not know God. If we love people because they love us, isn't that just like what lost people do? And if we greet our brothers only, meaning people who look like us, part of your family, people we like, if we greet those that we like only, isn't that what others do? We are not doing any more than people who don't know God.

Jesus' concluding remarks to his disciples: "Do not even the Gentiles (another word describing people who don't know God), don't even the Gentiles love like that?" You see, when the God of all grace captures our hearts, we start relating to others the way He relates to us.

"God shows His love for us in that while we were yet sinners…Christ died for us" (Romans 5:8). I love that verse, but there is a problem. We memorize it and we quote it, but we have little true understanding of its meaning. It's just a Bible verse. And so, if you don't mind, allow me to put the Burleson translation on it. We're going to look at this verse in this way. "Adam," and I'm just using a generic name. It could be Bill, could be Wade, Joe, I have no one in mind. "Adam shows his love to Beth" (again a generic name, could be Susie, Judy, whoever) but Beth commits adultery, yet all the time Beth is being unfaithful, Adam will do whatever it takes for his actions to be for Beth's good."

Now that's where the rubber meets the road. That's where the foot hits the gas pedal. That's where people really get upset, because we want to blame somebody else, anybody, or everybody for our pain. If only my husband would be like this, if only my wife would do that, if only they would be this way, we would be so happy.

I received a call this week from a gentleman and I could almost hear his tears coming through his voice. He had been utterly, completely rejected by his spouse. He then went through a long list of everything that needed to change in him. What he needed to do differently. What he hadn't been doing. What he should be doing. What he ought to be doing. At the end, he laughed till he could barely breathe, but I could hear his tears of rejection and defeat even in his laughter.

So, I talked him through some things. Do you know what I reminded him? I said, "Listen. If you are looking to your spouse for your sense of acceptance, you've got it all wrong. God is the One who is gracious to you when you are unworthy and undeserving. Your identity should come from His kindness to you, which is without strings because you've done nothing to cause Him to like you. And then when you are full of His grace, you can go back into a house where you are utterly rejected, and love the person rejecting you." You know what? He got it.

Certainly, what I'm writing is easy to teach on Sunday, but it's hard to live out on Monday. I get it. We need to have self-talks all the time. We've got to talk to ourselves about where our identity really comes from and remind ourselves that it comes from God. Problem is, we have such a screwed-up concept of who God is and why He loves us, we are performance-oriented in our relationship with God and we evaluate everybody around us on that same performance scale. But if we ever get captivated by God's grace, we will find ourselves extending that grace to the very people who are rejecting us.

When we awaken to the reality of favor without merit, change occurs. Many times we think that what we've got to do is lay down the law, or we've got to tell people where they're falling short in order for us to have a happy home and a happy life. But can we not see that that is selflove? In other words, when we are manipulating and controlling other people into conforming to a way that makes us happy, we are loving ourselves because we think if they change, we'll change for the better or look better. That's self-love. But if we ever grasp the fact that God loved us when we were unworthy, then we will begin to demonstrate love when other people around us are unworthy.

I'll never forget a show I once watched about a treatment center for anorexic and bulimic young women. This wasn't just any treatment center, though – this center boasts a 100% success rate with all of its clients. One hundred percent! When a young woman checks in, she is assigned at least one counselor, usually two or three. Around the clock, 24/7, during the days, weeks, and sometimes months, the young lady with an eating disorder is embraced physically. Counselors whisper into her ear words of acceptance, affirmation, and love. And those girls are healed.

Most of us have grown up in families or in relationships where it's all about performance. Our reality is constructed in the context of human relationships. The Scripture teaches us that there is eternal reality, a divine reality far more important than any human relationship that we might have. God's grace for us is that divine reality, and when we are captivated by His grace, we are changed from the inside out.

"Don't despise the riches of God's grace...for God's grace leads you to repentance" (Romans 2:4). It is God's grace that leads us to repentance (or to lasting change). We think that we are able to change people's lives by hammering the law. That doesn't change anyone. As an old British politician once said, "Men are hanged for stealing horses, not because of the crime. Men are hanged for stealing horses, that others may not steal horses." You see, the reason we are laying down the law to people around us is because we ourselves want them to change. The law with its condemnation controls people and enslaves them. Grace alone has the power to free people and transform them from the inside out. Let this sink in—the mindset of grace is "never worthy, always loved." Never worthy, always loved.

My husband will never be worthy, but he will always be loved. My wife will never be worthy, but she will always be loved. Why is that? Because that is exactly how God loves me. That is how God loves each one of us.

There is a difference between good judgment and living in judgment. If you are reading this and your husband is beating you, it is good judgment for you to leave the house, call the police and have your husband arrested, prosecuted, and sent to jail. That's good judgment. But as a child of God loving the unworthy, you are never to live in judgment of your husband. For example, your husband is a "couch potato" watching football games on a beautiful Saturday when you see so much opportunity for getting things done around the house. Can you work on those important projects without casting judgment on your husband? You are using "good judgment" in getting things done around the house on a beautiful day, but living "in judgment" is different than using good judgment.

As another example, if your son calls you and says "Mom, Dad, I need a hundred bucks," and you know he's a drug addict, it is good judgment to say to your son, "Son, we love you and whatever choices you make, we will always love you because that's the way God loves us. But we're not going to give you money because we believe in our good judgment it's not good for you or our family. But we love you, son." That's good judgment. But you'll never live in judgment as a graced person with those you love. Folks, this is so radical, but this is Christianity.

Luke 16:27–30: "Love your enemies, do good to those who hate you, bless those who curse you, pray for those who mistreat you. If someone slaps you on one cheek, turn to them the other also. If someone takes your coat, do not withhold your shirt from them. Give to everyone who asks you, and if anyone takes what belongs to you, do not demand it back."

What? Give to everyone who asks you, and if anyone takes what belongs to you, don't demand it back? What? Let me tell you something. You make a living by what you earn. You make a life by what you give. And if we ever want to know what it means to build a life with a legacy of grace, love people while bearing the mindset that they will never be worthy but they will always be loved, because that is exactly how the God of all grace loves me.

That's just part one of the five parts of the *Face of Grace*: the mind of grace. We'll next move to the mouth, and then we'll move to the eyes and the ears. By the way, for those of you who are theologians, these first five chapters are nothing but the doctrines of grace minus the theological words. I pray that through this series, all of our hearts will become captivated by the wonder of God's kindness, His benevolence, His unmerited favor toward us.

Chapter One Discussion Questions

1. How would you answer the question, "Who are you?"
2. What makes us worthy of God's grace?
3. Why is it easier to accept God's grace when we are at the end of ourselves, "on our backs looking up to Him"?
4. As Christians, what keeps us from living as people of grace?

Chapter Two

"Never Desiring; Always Chosen"

John 13:34
"Jesus said, 'Love one another as I have loved you.'"

When we were born, all of us started out as just a little baby human being. Science tells us that there is a place in the frontal lobe of our mind that arouses delight when we see a person's face. That place in the frontal lobe is called the *fusiform gyrus*. Any time a baby sees a face, happiness and pleasure sweep onto the baby's expression. That is not by accident.

Try this sometime. Those of you who are new parents, get in front of your child and put yourself right in front of their eyes. Notice your baby's reaction when they see your face. God has designed us from the beginning to the end of life, to recognize human faces. In fact, I could do a test right now and show you two profiles of the same face. Within a millisecond, you would know that it's one face seen from two different angles because God has gifted you that way.

We're asking the question, "What is the face of grace?" The Bible says that our God is the God of all grace. If that's the case and you've been born again as the Apostle John describes it, *by the God of all grace*, then that means you should reflect grace in terms of your identity because the nature of grace in your Heavenly Father is now within you.

If you know God, if you've been born again by the Spirit, if Jesus Christ is your Savior, then you should reflect your Father's face. He is the God of all grace. But what does that look like?

I said previously that a graced person has a mind that thinks of God's favor and love toward us in terms of "Never Worthy, Always

Loved." Consequently, every time graced people (saved people) meet another person, *we do not think* about whether they are good or not, whether they're worthy or not. We think to ourselves, "You know, that person may never be worthy, but I will love them anyway, because that is exactly how the God of all grace regards me. I am never worthy enough, and I'll never be able to perform well enough, but God loves me anyway."

I want to continue describing this mind of grace in a follower of Jesus by showing you that those of us who have experienced God's grace should have:

A mind that thinks about other people,
Never Desiring, Always Chosen

Here's what I mean by that. Those of us who have lived any number of years as adults have experienced relationships with people that turn away from us. They don't like us anymore. They're tired of the way we talk. They're tired of the things we do. They despise our habits that they used to think were cute, so they walk away from the relationship. Maybe it's the case where we have a relationship with a friend, and all of a sudden, they begin doing things that turn us off, so we turn away. I want to show you that grace does the exact opposite. Grace chooses to pursue, even when the person you are in relationship with turns away from you.

Be careful here. We are not talking about pursuit that is based upon self-love. That's the type of pursuing you find in Hollywood. That's fatal attraction. Some of you may recall the movie *Fatal Attraction* starring Michael Douglas, where the girlfriend of the married man (played by Michael Douglas) wanted him. She desired him, so she pursued him. That's not the kind of pursuit we are talking about, because that pursuit is based on self-gratification. That kind of pursuit is destructive. A graced person will pursue relationship, even when people turn away, but it is for the other person's good, not their own. That's exactly what God does for us.

Here's what God says of His people. "I will heal their waywardness; I will love them freely" (Hosea 14:4). You can't heal a wayward person without going toward them, because they are estranged. When you experience the grace of God and are captivated by Him and His grace for you, then you will move toward other people even when they don't like you. That's exactly what God does for you. God moved toward you even when you were disinterested or even moving in the other direction, away from Him.

I realize that many of you may have grown up in a church where you were taught just the opposite. You were told at the church you attended that there were certain things that you had to do in order for a Holy God to even begin to like you. Depending upon the denomination, these steps vary. In one church, there are seven steps to God. For the typical Baptist church, it's usually just one step, but it's that long step down an aisle at the end of a service while people around you are singing "Just As I Am." In some churches it's a long "invitation" where you were told repeatedly by the pastor you must "do this" or God will have nothing to do with you.

That's just not what the Bible teaches. "There is no one who seeks God, no, not one" (Romans 3:11). Now, if you're seeking the Lord right now, if you are pursuing Him, you're probably thinking to yourself, "Well, wait! I'm an illustration of someone seeking God. What does that verse mean, 'Nobody seeks God, no not one?'" Just this: you were running from God, and He pursued you. "We love Him, (the Bible says) because He first loved us" (I John 4:19).

A grace relationship doesn't think about the love of the other person. No, no, no. In a grace relationship where the graced person is pursuing, we go after people. We go after them the way God went after us. Another verse, God speaking, "I have loved you with an everlasting love; and with lovingkindness have I drawn you" (Jeremiah 31:3). That's powerful. How about this one? The Psalmist said, "He reached down from on high and took hold of me; He drew me out of deep waters" (Psalm 18:16). That's grace!

You say, "Pastor, every time I've gone to church, the teacher, the preacher, the Sunday School teacher, leadership, everybody always talked about my love for God. My commitment to God. What I needed to promise God. I'm a little uncomfortable, because now here you are talking about *God's* love for *me*. You're talking about His grace, His kindness for me, an unworthy person, somebody who's not seeking Him. I don't know how to respond to that." Point well taken. I get it.

In fact, a few years ago Bill McCartney, head football coach for the Colorado Buffaloes started Promise Keepers. Our church really wasn't heavily involved in it, but it was a great movement. In Promise Keepers, men met in stadiums all over the country singing worship songs and recommitting their lives to Christ, while making new pledges to God in a spirit of renewal and accountability. I'm not going to denigrate what they did because it was a very positive movement overall. But I was asked one time, "Pastor, why is our church not involved with Promise Keepers?" My response was, "When the name is changed to The Promise Keeper, we'll get involved because I want people to be captivated by the One who pursues sinners in incredible love."

Do you get that? The power of Promise Keepers in my opinion, comes from God, The Promise Keeper. The Bible tells us, "All people are liars" (Psalm 116:11), so we better trust in the God of all grace and not our promises. When I get captivated by Him and His love for me, then I will be able to convey that same kind of love and grace to others, even liars.

The Bible says, "This is love: not that we love God, but that He loves us and sent His Son to rescue us" (I John 4:10.) Do you believe that? Are you captivated by the love and the grace of God for you? Do you believe He pursues you in love and kindness and grace even when you are not caring for Him, even when you are running from Him? Do you believe His love for you endures even when you do things that you know bother you so much, they've got to bother Him to the point He's done with you? Do you believe that? How do you know if you really, truly believe that? There's one way you can know. You go after people who do things that bother other people. Do you go after people who are running from you, and for their good?

In Psalm 139 from the New American Standard Version, we see the incredible, almost unfathomable grace of God for you. He is the God of all grace. Let me show you how He pursues you. Are you ready for this? Hang on. Fasten your seat belts, because this is amazing.

David writes in Psalm 139:1, "O Lord, you have searched me and known me." You remember David, King of Israel. Scripture records that he had done some things that really no King should ever be proud of doing. No man would ever want a record of these deeds to be recorded for posterity; in fact, we would rather these things that bring shame be erased and never mentioned. But the Bible records David's actions, and in this verse he says, "O Lord," followed by God's personal name, which in Hebrew is Yahweh. "Yahweh, you have searched me, and you know me."

Do you see the word *search* there? It's a particular Hebrew word which means to *diligently probe*. Let me describe this word for you. We get up fairly early every weekday morning because Rachelle and I both work. I study at home in the morning while Rachelle is getting ready for work, then I'll take her. For two mornings on the weekend, Rachelle can sleep a little bit later. On Sunday mornings typically I will get up at 4:30 or 5 o'clock, but I want my wife to continue sleeping, so I will get ready in the dark. Do you have any idea how hard it is to find black socks when it's dark in your bedroom? So, what do I do? I get my phone. That's right. I turn the little flashlight on, I pull open my drawer very quietly and I shine that light into my sock drawer, looking diligently, probing for a pair of black socks. Sometimes I don't find any, and instead I get a mismatched burgundy and blue pair of socks. God shines a light into the sock drawer of your soul and knows what's there; no surprises.

So, this is what God does to you. He probes you. He searches you. He shines His spotlight on you. In fact, if you go on in verses 2 through 6, David describes how well God knows him. "When I awaken, You know everything about me. When I go out for a walk, You are there along the path. When I'm trying to even form a word, before it gets on my tongue, You know what I'm going to say. You know what I'm thinking. That wisdom, that knowledge is too marvelous for me. I can't even attain it." By the way, nobody knows you that well but God. Nobody! And He knows everything about you because He has probed you.

What do you want to do when people know you as you really are? Let me put it like this. Let's say that everything you thought, everything you thought about doing and intended to do but didn't, every word you wanted to say but didn't say, every word you did say and wished you hadn't, every action of your life, everything for the last seven days about you: thoughts, intents of your heart, actions of your life, those things you did in secret and in public…Everything! In thirty seconds, all would be displayed on- screen in full living color for everyone to see. How would you feel? What would you want to do? Run? Hide? By the way, that's why people at church never really share what's going on in their lives, because churches seem to develop programs that alienate people who feel as though they don't measure up.

That's why one of the greatest ministries we have is Celebrate Recovery. If you go there and you are struggling with anything in your life, with hurts, habits, or addictions, you sit down, introduce yourself and you say "Hi, I am Wade Burleson, I am struggling with ..." and then you name it. You can be "real" there because we've taught people in Celebrate Recovery to warmly embrace those who are known for who they really are.

But here in Psalm 139, David thinks about God and how much God knows him, and he says, "When I think about that, I want to run." That's verse 7. "Where can I go to flee from Your Spirit? Where can I hide from Your presence?" Look what he says. "If I make my bed in heaven, You are there. If I make my bed in hell, You are there. If I pick up wings like a bird and I fly to the uttermost parts of the sea..." (like Majuro, where our missionary serves in the Pacific, way out there in the middle of nowhere), "God is there!"

When I get so tired of being known like that, I think to myself, "I don't want to get out of bed, so I'm going to pull the covers over me and let the darkness hide me from You." That's right there in Psalm 139. David says, "You are there," verse 12, "darkness is not dark to You, even the night is as bright as the day. I can't hide, for You formed me in my mother's womb. You fearfully and wonderfully made me. You know everything about me, You wrought me in the depths of my mom's womb." None of us can hide from our Creator God.

By the way, I read a lot, and right now I'm reading about DNA. Now I am not a scientist, nor do I have a degree in science. But I'm reading Dr. Francis Collins and I'm reading about the new discoveries made in the last ten years about DNA. If you are like me having gone to college in the eighties, being taught evolution and that people evolved from amoebas, and you believed that, get a grip. Get a grip, because what science is discovering now is that every cell in your body is programmed with three billion parts of DNA. Every speck of you, every little piece of DNA was intentionally designed by God, and you are who you are because God fearfully and wonderfully made you, therefore you cannot hide from Him.

When David realizes this, and he's not been a stellar individual, he comes to a conclusion that we read in verse 17. If there is any verse that I could convince you to memorize from the Old Testament, it would be this verse. It's like the John 3:16 of the Old Testament. In verse 17, David says "How precious are your thoughts about me, O God." That's grace.

Let me show you what the word *precious* means here. It's the Hebrew word for *rare*. It's like the inscription underneath the Ben Johnson diamond in the British museum. The inscription says: "O rare Ben Johnson diamond." That's the word translated *precious*. "How precious Lord are your thoughts to me." Why is the Ben Johnson diamond rare? Rare because there are very few of them. So, in this case is David saying that God doesn't have very many thoughts about him? And is this what you think about God? Do you think that God never thinks about you? That He's got way too many other people to worry about? I mean, He's got the President. He's got world leaders. Can He really be bothered thinking about little old me? As I'm changing my kid's diapers, as I'm doing the dishes, as I'm working the yard or paying the bills, God doesn't have any time for me. Is that what you think?

That's not what David is saying. Go on in verse 18 and he says, "If I were to count the number of your thoughts toward me, they would number more than the sands of the seashore." Next time you are on the beach and you're kicking some sand with your sandals, or you're making a sand castle, why don't you just think about the fact that the thoughts of God toward you number more than the sands of that beach on which you are playing.

So, God's thoughts toward you are not rare in *number*. How are they rare, then? I hope you're ready for this, because this is what is so cool. No one else in your life *probes* you and *knows* you, *pursues* you in grace, and although knowing you inside and out, embraces you and *loves* you. God is kind to you even when you weren't seeking Him, even when you had no thoughts of Him, and even when you were doing some things that irritate you and your family. In your mind these things obviously have to irritate God, and yet...

How precious God's thoughts are toward you! His thoughts are rare in nature. Nobody else loves you like that. Now I know you want to be loved like that, but you'll never find a spouse, you'll never find a friend, you'll never find anybody who loves you like that, not even a mom or a dad. We are so programmed in our fallen nature to love people because of what they've done to us and for us, we cannot fathom that somebody would love us and give to us, needing nothing in return and regardless of all the wrongs we've done.

You see, there's one great hindrance to resting in the glorious love of God that I just described—your human relationships. Believe it or not, that's what holds you back. You ask, what do you mean? Well, what one feels by touch (that's the flesh) is easier to believe than what one hears by teaching (that's faith).

Let me show you what I mean. The only thing that will ever change you is this: becoming captivated by the grace of God. You will not change through rules and regulations. You will not change with the belief that God will move toward you when you are good enough.

You will not change by believing that God is gracious to you and kind to you because of your promises and your pledges. You will only change when you are captivated by the God of all grace Who holds precious thoughts toward you, even when you run from Him and do things that irritate yourself.

I have believed what I'm teaching you for all of my life. When I was a pastor in Tulsa, I was trying to teach it and it was hard. It was an inner-city church with very traditional ways, and I was young. It was difficult, but God gave me a number of circumstances to show His grace, to live it and not just teach it.

One day I'll never forget is the day I met Eric Wolf. Eric has given me permission to tell his story. One day he was driving by our church ready to commit suicide. He had a gun in his seat and he was drinking alcohol, trying to numb his feelings so he could pull the trigger. He saw our church sign, and something grabbed him and he said, "I don't know what it was, but I turned in because I wanted to meet the people who put what they put on the sign." I don't remember what was on the sign, but what I do remember is what happened when Eric saw it. Eric came in and met Jeff Hatcher our worship pastor, and Jeff led him to faith in Christ. It was about a two-hour meeting. Jeff simply talked with Eric about the love of God toward man. By the time I met Eric, he had already opened his life to Christ and he was just beaming. He was radiating. It was like the weight of the world had been taken off his shoulders. Nobody had ever told him before that God loved him and had actually pursued him.

He said, "What do I do next?" I said, "Eric, next Sunday come to church and just tell people how you've given your life to Christ and how you've been captivated by His love, and we'll baptize you." I explained baptism to him. That next Sunday Eric came bounding down the aisle, so happy, literally dancing. I put my arm around him and I introduced him to the church, saying, "Folks, this is Eric Wolf. This past week he was going to take his life. God saved him. God convinced him that He loved him, that He gave His Son to deliver him." Then as I had my arm around him, I looked and saw that Eric had on a Budweiser, King of Beers, T- shirt.

An old deacon on the front row noticed Eric's shirt. I love this man, but he was traditional. He had been raised in a church of works where it was all about what you did for God and committed to God. I could see he was frowning. He came up to me afterwards and said, "Pastor, did you talk to Eric?" I said, "About what?" pretending I didn't know. "Did you talk to Eric about that beer tee shirt? That boy should know better. He should never have come into this church wearing that tee shirt" (Sigh). I called the deacon by name and said, "Listen. I'm not going to talk to Eric." That took a lot of courage for a young pastor to say that to a deacon in his eighties who in fact happened to be Chairman of the Deacons. They could have fired me. "I'm not going to talk to Eric about his tee shirt. Let me tell you why. If I tell Eric to take that tee shirt off, then he's going to be convinced that the love of God is based upon what Eric does. I've got to help Eric be captivated by the love of God, independent of Eric's performance. And then when he's captivated by God's grace and love, Eric will change from the inside out on his own, not because of law."

The deacon just looked at me as if to say, I don't want a message, I just want you to fix him. He simply turned around and walked away. There was something about Eric that none of us knew about him, but God knew. Eric was a beer tee shirt collector. Every single Sunday Eric came with a different beer tee shirt. Beers from Czechoslovakia, beers from Germany, beers I didn't know about. Every Sunday, Eric Wolf came to church sporting a beer tee shirt, until about eight weeks later he came to church and was proudly wearing a tee shirt that says Jesus Christ, King of Kings.

I said, "Eric what a great shirt, where did you get that?" He said, "You won't believe it. They have Christian tee shirt stores out there." Now let me finish the story. Eric is now in the United States military, married, with kids of his own. And when we moved to Enid to become pastor of Emmanuel, his aunt was a member of this church. My point to you is this: had we not pursued Eric the way God pursues us, full of grace, full of kindness, embracing the unworthy, pursuing people when they don't even know what it means to pursue others, I'm not sure Eric would be where he is today.

I want to convince you in this series that because life often deals us a great deal of hurt, the only person who can heal our hurt is the Lord Jesus Christ, who is our Balm in Gilead. There is an old saying that if you don't heal the hurt that is in you, you will bleed over people who never cut you. I'm convinced that until we are captivated by the love of God for us as described in Psalm 139, we will never be able to move toward people the way God has moved toward us.

I talked about Psalm 139 from the Old Testament, and now I want to show you a couple of verses of Scripture from the New Testament. Paul prays "that you, firmly fixed in love yourselves, may be able to grasp (with all Christians) how wide and deep and long and high is the love of God" (Ephesians 3:17-18). What a wonderful prayer. Do you grasp the love of God like that? "(And I pray) that you will know for yourselves that love which is so far beyond our comprehension…so that you will be filled with God himself" (Ephesians 3:19)!

He is the God of all grace. God's choice to pursue you, once you begin to understand this, will captivate you. Then when you are captivated by His grace for your life, the understanding of His free love for you will empower you to love other people in the same manner.

Never Desiring; Always Chosen

Let me remind you. Be careful that you don't confuse your work for a business or company, and your job performance for a salary, with the principles of grace in relationships. We can all be gracious with the people we work with and with our families and friends, but we perform at work for pay. We don't work by grace. For example: I work for my church. They pay my salary. I wish there were a day where they didn't pay me a dime, and that day may come, but I do work for them and it's very difficult. It's difficult to do what I do. Extremely hard. But you know what? If I don't do a good job, they have every right to fire me. Period. End of sentence, end of story.

But if they fire me, I am obligated by the God of all grace to love them where they are. You see, the test of whether or not I am captivated by the grace of God is my ability to love people even when they run from me, even when they mistreat me, even when they say hurtful things against me. Would I do one of their spouse's funerals if I wasn't paid a salary? That's a test. Would I come to their home when they are in marital conflict, without being paid a salary? That's another test. Would I visit them in the hospital? That too is a test. All these are tests of whether I live the grace that I teach.

As a reminder, your marriage is not an employment contract. Your marriage is supposed to be based upon grace. "A new command I give you," Jesus says, "love one another as I have loved you" (John 13:34). Can you love somebody the way God loves you? It's a choice.

Some of you who have been trained in theology understand the doctrines of grace. There are five of them. These first five chapters are nothing but taking those doctrines of grace, taking out the theological terms, and just writing to you as a friend. **"Never Worthy; Always Loved"** is consistent with the doctrine that Christians have historically called Total Depravity. **"Never Desir-**

ing, Always Chosen" is consistent with the biblical doctrine called Unconditional Election.

These two principles convey how God thinks about you and why it is in God's nature to love you. My prayer is that you will be captivated by it so that you can love the people around you in the same manner.

Chapter Two Discussion Questions

1. What does it mean to "pursue somebody the way God pursues us"?
2. How do you pursue somebody that seems to be very different from you? For example, lives a different lifestyle, holds differing values, or is unlikeable?
3. What does being "captivated by God's grace" mean to you?
4. According to this chapter, how can we reflect God's grace to others?

Chapter Three

"Never Perfect; Always Embraced"

Romans 8:29

"For those God foreloved, He also predestined to be conformed to the image of His Son."

Years ago, I used to have a license plate on the back of my car that read KERUSSO, which in Greek means *I Preach*. One day I pulled into the parking lot of Will Rogers International Airport, got my bags out of the trunk, and boarded one of those shuttles. After getting on and putting my bags up, I noticed that two women were staring at me. I looked away, and a few seconds later looked back. They were still staring at me. I asked, "Can I help you?" To my surprise, they replied, "Would you sing us a song?" It was then I realized they had probably seen my license plate. I asked, "Why do you want me to sing you a song?" One said, "Aren't you the Italian opera singer Caruso?" Not long after this incident, I took that license plate off the back of my car.

I've been in the airport at least a half-dozen times and people have stopped me to ask if I was Mitt Romney. No joke. I don't think that I look like Mitt Romney, but somebody apparently does. No, no, I'm not Mitt Romney. So, I've been mistaken for a singer because of my license plate and I've been mistaken for a politician because people thought I looked like him, but when asked about it, I always correct their mistakes.

I want to ask you a question now. Why did sinners want to be around Jesus back in the day, but not so much around Jesus' followers today? If you doubt that sinners liked being around Jesus, all you have to do is read the New Testament. The adulteress was rescued by Jesus. The tax collectors who were hated by the religious, invited Jesus to dine with them. The lepers whom nobody wanted to be around, Jesus embraced. We find the woman at the well, a lady who had been married five times and was living with a man who was not her husband, in deep conversation with the Messiah. Everyone else rejected this woman, but not Jesus. Why is it that sinners wanted to be around Jesus then, but not so much around us nowadays? Could it be because we don't look like Jesus anymore?

Here's an example of Christians today that don't look at all like Jesus. I once saw a photo of a man holding two signs. One read "God Hates Fags" and the other read "Fags Die God Laughs." The man was Fred Phelps, Pastor of Westboro Baptist Church in Kansas. You might remember Westboro Baptist Church from news reports a few years ago; it's a church known for its inflammatory hate speech against homosexuals and LGBT+ people. Fred and his church members picketed our church a few years ago. Once when I did a funeral for a military serviceman, they came down from Kansas to picket us.

Churches like Westboro give other churches a bad name. A few years ago, we suffered a fire at Emmanuel where our sign outside the church caught fire. I got a phone call: "Pastor, the sign is on fire!" I asked, "What do you mean the sign is on fire? The billboard out south?" "No, no, no, the casino sign, it's on fire!" meaning, the digital sign out front. Fire trucks were arriving because part of our church sign was on fire, but only the word *Baptist* was on fire. The sign was made of metal, so the fire melted *that one word.* We contemplated putting the word Baptist back up, but it would have cost several thousand dollars, and in the end we decided to leave only the name

Emmanuel on the sign. One of the factors that went into the decision is the fact that the meaning of the word Baptist has been hijacked.

I'm a Baptist theologian and third generation Baptist preacher. I write books about Baptist history. I know what Baptists have believed throughout our tenure as a denomination. We have a delightful heritage of grace, but it's been hijacked by people like Fred Phelps. One of these days if we ever get our name back, we'll proudly put it back up on the sign, but we don't want nonbelievers driving by our church, seeing the word Baptist and thinking, "Oh, I want nothing to do with those people because they don't want anything to do with me." Could this be because they sense that we don't see them as Jesus sees them?

There are a lot of people who say that they are Christian, but all that gets portrayed is hate and judgment and fighting. I think when you ponder the question of why sinners wanted to be around Jesus then, but maybe not so much us today, you will come to the conclusion that Jesus is a picture of the face of grace, and we seem to have lost it. Let me show you what I mean.

In the Bible, God our Father is called the God of all grace and He calls us. When we read the New Testament, those of us who have come to faith in the God of all grace recognize what He's done for us in the Lord Jesus Christ, and we realize we are called to live a life consistent with our calling of grace. In other words, we learn that we should look like Jesus. We should live a life that reflects the image of the God of all grace. It seems what has happened in our modern day is that evangelical Christians, those of us who call ourselves followers or disciples of Jesus Christ, do not exhibit grace.

Thus far, we've looked at how a graced person thinks. When we have been graced by God, called by the God of all grace, our thinking begins to change. We think to ourselves, "You know what, I'll never be worthy of God's love, but He loves me anyway. Therefore, I'm going to be consistent with the calling I have from the God of all grace, and I'm going to love the unworthy as I am loved."

We've also seen how we don't really seek God but how He chooses us. He pursues us. And when we begin to understand that we love Him because He first loved us, then all of a sudden when people turn away from us, we're not going to get angry, we're just going to pursue them in relationship for their good, because that's how God pursues us.

Continuing along these lines, if we truly wish to reflect Jesus in this world, you and I need to have:

A mind that thinks,

Never Perfect, Always Embraced

This is so contrary to most church teachings. It may even be opposite to the way that you were raised, and the reason is because perfection is the standard that every one of us strives to attain. We want to be perfect. We want to have the perfect marriage, the perfect kids, the perfect church, the perfect pastor. We want perfect relationships, perfect friendships. That's the standard, isn't it? I believe it is. You know how perfection is defined? Perfection is defined as "the condition, state, or quality of being free from all flaws or defects."

We live in a culture that promotes perfection. A good example can be found in kids who play video games. What do they do when they get to the second level and they've got black marks against them? They quit and go back to the first level. Why? Because it's easier to start all over and blow away the game where they failed. So that's what they do, because we're trained to think that it's got to be perfect or it's not worth keeping. It's got to be perfect or I will not embrace it.

Never Perfect; Always Embraced

I did a funeral this past week for a gentleman by the name of Squire Utsler. Squire was a wonderful man, a rare breed. I don't do funerals like his very much anymore. Squire was in his nineties, a WWII hero, he danced with Betty Grable, he played as an extra in the movie The Fighting Seabees, and he knew John Wayne. I mean, this man lived! It was a wonderful memorial that we celebrated that day. Dorothy, his wife, is still living. They had just celebrated 73 years of marriage and I asked, "Dorothy, how did you and Squire do it? How did you last for 73 years?" Here's what she said: "You know, our marriage wasn't perfect, not even close. We just didn't quit."

Let me ask you a question. Have you come to the place in your life where you realize God hasn't quit on you? The only way you will understand this is when you understand the mind of God, which is the mind of grace. He is the God of all grace, and the mind of grace thinks "Never perfect; always embraced." Now the reason you don't hear it in churches is because pastors will come across a verse like this one where Jesus says, "You are to be perfect, as your heavenly Father is perfect" (Matthew 5:48). Most pastors will wax eloquent on that verse and basically instruct, "God is perfect and He demands that you be perfect." Every person knows he or she is not perfect, and if you don't think this to be true, there are more problems in your life than you realize. But because we hear the message to "be perfect because God is perfect," we think that God is like our earthly father, expecting perfection from us.

If you grew up in western Oklahoma, you know that they are among some of the toughest, hardest working men in the world. There is an old saying that a western Oklahoma farmer would love you so much he would almost tell you that he loved you. That's the way some of us grew up. That's a tall order to measure up to, so we had to work hard and we had to do it just right. Basically, we've got to be perfect and if we weren't, perhaps we felt the anger, the wrath, the turning away of our earthly father. We later grew to think that's what God does to us. No, no, no. It's just the opposite. We will never meet God's standard of perfection, but He always embraces us. Instead of demanding perfection, He gives to us the gift of perfection in His Son.

"Here's a trustworthy saying worthy of (your) full acceptance, Christ came to save sinners" (I Timothy 1:15). We quote that verse, but we forget that Christ came because He was sent by the God of all grace, your Creator. Out of His love for you, He provided in His Son the perfection you needed, and embraced the imperfect you, giving you all the gifts of grace. Wow! "This is love; not that we loved God but that He loved us and sent His Son for us" (I John 4:10). You see, the mind of grace thinks, "Never perfect, always embraced." "It is God who is working in you, both to will and to work to fulfill His good purpose" (Philippians 2:13).

I can guess what many of you are thinking right now. That's hard for you to accept because maybe you have a son who struggles with alcoholism, or you've got a daughter and she's just "come out" and told you she's a lesbian. You've got a friend who's got a drug addiction. You can't embrace people like that, or you don't even feel you should, or you can't wrap your mind around it. I know. I know. No judgment. No judgment against you at all. What I am proposing to you is that the reason it's difficult for you to embrace imperfect people is because you've never considered that God embraces you as imperfect. You see, God embraces us as imperfect because He *needs nothing* from us.

I want you to think about something for a moment. I want you to think about a person that you once turned away from, a person that you have rejected. Or on the flip side, think about a person in your life who has turned away from you and rejected you. Why? I would propose to you that the rejection of imperfect people comes because we needed something from them, and they didn't come through for us. As a mom, you need a son who looks good to your friends. As a wife, you need a husband who looks good to your family. As a husband, you need friends who either look good or make you look good. Then, when people fail you, when people don't measure up to the way you want them to be, there's a tendency to turn away.

Thankfully, God doesn't do that to you. "I have no need (God says) …of your sacrifices…or your gifts" (Psalm 50:9–12). That's stunning! When we begin to understand that this is how God embraces us, that our Creator is truly on our side, it is the embrace of grace. It has nothing to do with the standard of perfection, for He has provided that standard for us in His Son. When we come to faith in Christ, the embrace of God is ours without condition. We can't imagine the feeling of being loved without condition. Embraced without caveat. Accepted with no qualifications.

I tell people all the time that the longest eighteen inches in life are those eighteen inches from the head and the mind to the heart. I can tell you what God thinks of you. I can tell you how He pursues you. I can tell you that He embraces you. But it's like "I don't feel it. I don't feel it." I know. I understand. Sometimes you have to see it modeled in the human realm, and that's very rare among us Christians. It's any wonder that everybody liked to hang around Jesus, but few people like to hang around us.

God says, "I have loved you with an everlasting love; I have drawn you with unfailing kindness" (Jeremiah 31:3). I believe that until we comprehend God's embrace of us through grace, we will struggle to embrace the imperfect people in our own lives.

Here's another verse, "Out of His fullness we have all received grace in place of grace already given" (John 1:16). This is a good verse for us to memorize. We only think about the grace of God in terms of being saved from hell, but Paul says, "Oh no, out of His fullness in coming to an understanding of His grace in my life now, I receive grace in place of grace. I grow in grace and the knowledge of it." You see, what happens is this: the more you begin to discover who God is in your life, the more you are filled with all the fullness of the God of all grace. When this happens, you can't help but have that grace leak/spread out to others. The Bible says that God is "conforming us into the image of His Son" (Romans 8:29). One of the reasons why people liked hanging around Jesus but not much around us is because they saw grace on the face of Jesus, and they don't see it so much on our faces.

Let me give you an illustration, a story. In 2002 I was surprisingly elected president of the Baptist General Convention of Oklahoma (BGCO). I wasn't even running, yet at the convention that year they elected me. During my first week on the job, I received a phone call from a woman. She said, "Reverend Burleson, I see that you now represent Baptists from across the state of Oklahoma. I'm the head of Soul Force, that is the lesbian and homosexual activist group, and we believe Baptists are so full of hate, so angry, are so prudish with their thoughts about homosexuality and lesbianism, we are going to come picket your church because you now represent the entire Baptist denomination. But before we do, we'd like to meet with you." I immediately replied, "Sure," and we set an appointment.

I drove down to Shawnee, Oklahoma to meet with Soul Force, and I walked into a room with my friend Buddy Hunt who was vice-president of the BGCO at the time.

In the room were tables arranged in a horseshoe shape, and seated were probably about a dozen lesbian women and about half dozen homosexual men. They were all in the leadership of Oklahoma Soul

Force. We sat down and they each very briefly introduced themselves, taking no more than a few seconds apiece.

I wanted to know more; I wanted to know their names and get acquainted. So, I stopped them and said, "Wait. Can we go back to the first and will you give me your first and last name, then will you just tell me a little bit about yourself?" So, they went back and started over willingly but rather hesitantly. I'm usually pretty good at names because I work at it, so I wrote down their names and then I listened to their stories. The pain was palpable in that room. I heard young men say that they had been raised in foster homes, and many of them had been sexually abused. I heard young women say that their own families had rejected them, and a couple of them had been adopted and didn't even know their own families.

As they went one by one, I probed and asked more questions just to get to know them better. We got about halfway through when the young woman that was speaking began to cry, saying, "The only person who's really ever accepted me is my mother, and she's dying of cancer." I asked her mother's name, and after she told me I addressed the group. "You know what, would you all mind if we just all stood up and we held hands and we prayed for her mother?" They said, "Sure." So, we all stood up, held hands and I led us in prayer for her mother. Then we sat back down and finished going through the introductions.

The introductions alone took an hour and a half, and the meeting was scheduled for a total of two hours. By the end of the meeting I was able to call them all by name, and they were able to call me by name. The leader, the woman who had called me finally said, "Well, Reverend Burleson, this was surprising. We really didn't expect you to care for us as people. But why don't we get down to business. You're the president of the Baptist Convention; do you believe homosexuality and lesbianism is a sin?" I said, "Well, yes." And they said, "Well, we want to change your mind. And the way we're going to do it, we're going to come and we're going to picket your church a week from Sunday." I replied, "Okay. Let me just tell you a couple of things. First, I would never have come in here and declared to you that I believe homosexuality and lesbianism is a sin. Why would I do that? But, you asked me, so I responded.

"And here's the second thing. Enid, OK is a long way away from where we are in Shawnee, and you are going to have a hundred and fifty to two hundred people come to petition us. You're going to have to travel on Saturday to get there early on Sunday morning. Listen, don't get a hotel. We've got a very generous church. We will open up our homes and you can stay in our homes free of charge. Our host and hostess for the church, Doug and Peggy, will make you an incredible breakfast. Now, we've got three services, so you want to get there about 7:30 a.m. and we will feed you breakfast. And I tell you what, we've got a main thoroughfare, Highway 412, right in front of the church, so don't go park across the street. You just come and park where we park. Bring your signs and you can picket there in the parking lot; it's a lot safer."

They looked at me like, "Are you kidding?" I replied, "No. No. I'm serious. I've gotten to know you. I love you. I'm praying for the healing of your mom. You can come and picket. We'd love to have you." The meeting ended, and wouldn't you know, they never came to picket Emmanuel.

That's not the end of the story. The following summer, the Southern Baptist Convention was being held in St. Louis, Missouri. There, in front of the convention center in downtown St. Louis was Soul Force. They had come from around the nation to be there. It looked and sounded like a riot. There were Christians yelling at homosexuals and lesbians, and activists who were yelling back at Christians. You saw Baptist preachers and their wives walking by and praying down the imprecatory Psalms (psalms that ask God to destroy enemies) on these lesbians and homosexuals, scowling at them, sneering and so on. As my wife and I approached the convention center, Rachelle said, "What in the world is going on over there?" I wasn't really sure.

At about that very moment I recognized that it was Soul Force, and a couple of people from within that group called out, "Pastor Wade, Pastor Wade, come over here." Oh, you should have seen the look on all the Baptist preachers' faces around me! Rachelle and I went over to the group. They put down their signs and stopped their yelling. Soul Force members who knew us from Oklahoma introduced us to other members from around the nation. I hugged them and they hugged me in return. As Baptists were walking by, they were wondering what on earth was going on! I'll tell you what it was. It was somebody embracing someone else with grace.

The story doesn't end there. Just a few months ago, fifteen years after I met with this group, I received an email from a woman who was in that original meeting, a lesbian who had now been diagnosed with terminal cancer, and she had questions about eternity. This lady wrote, "Pastor Wade, you're the Christian that I wanted to ask, how can I be ready to meet God?"

May I propose to you that when the New Testament says, "be ready to give an answer for the hope that is within you," have you ever noticed that we are to be ready to give an answer *when asked?* You see, Christians today who don't look like Jesus are giving answers to questions that have never been asked. But if we ever have the face of grace and just stay with people where they are, they may start asking us questions that we can then answer with truth and grace.

It's possible you're thinking to yourself: We need rules, we need standards, we need the law. Yes, we need standards, in fact we hold the Bible as our standard. However, we don't use the Bible as a Billy club against others that "don't measure up". No, no, no. Let me tell you what happens. When you hit people with the law and standards and rules, they will either run from you or hide from you. Instead, if you'll embrace people, even people who reject you, even people who are imperfect, people who are close to you who have made very poor decisions, it's the embrace of grace that will ultimately lead them to ask questions of the hope that is within you.

I've answered why sinners don't want to be around us too much while they did want to be around Jesus. It's because we don't look like our Daddy. I'm asking you to have a mind that thinks, "Never Perfect, Always Embraced." It becomes less important to dwell on what people do to us, and more important to simply embrace the imperfect with grace because that is exactly how God has embraced us. The only way this can be done is when divine grace fills our hearts.

Chapter Three Discussion Questions

1. We strive for perfection, even though God doesn't demand it from us. Why is this?
2. If we're focused on perfection, how does that hinder us reaching others for Christ?
3. The lady at Soul Force contacted Pastor Wade when she was diagnosed with terminal cancer, asking him how she could be ready to meet God. Why do you think she felt comfortable contacting Pastor Wade, versus another Christian closer to home?
4. As believers, we are "Never Perfect; Always Embraced." How can we live this out to those around us, especially non-believers?

Chapter Four

"Never Seeking; Always Pursued"

Ephesians 2:5

"God made us alive with Christ when we were dead in transgressions."

When you leave a room, you leave some trace evidence of your presence in that room. In your chair might be a skin cell, possibly a hair follicle, something from your body. It is part of you, your DNA. In fact, it is called deoxyribonucleic acid. That's the official name for DNA, and that is your code. That is who you are.

When police go to a crime scene, they don protective covering and collect specimens containing deoxyribonucleic acid in order to identify the criminal. You see, there is no other human being that carries that person's DNA. Just the same, nobody else carries your DNA, either. You are unique. To further drive this point home, think of it this way: every cell of your body contains three billion particles of the code that makes you, you.

Let me illustrate. When you turn on your computer, you have many programs that come up on your home screen. Possibly Microsoft Word will be on your desktop. That's a program to help you write. Kindle may be on your desktop. That's a program for reading books on your computer. Every program on your computer has a code behind it. A designer coded the program that you use with every computer application. For those of you that are in high school, college, or university studying for a degree, you often have professors who are liable to teach that you are the product of accident, that you exist by chance, that all of us evolve from an amoeba as genes merely fighting to survive, and it's just by chance that we happen to be here today.

Truth is, that "chance" just "doesn't happen". It cannot happen. The odds of that happening are the same as you waking up tomorrow morning, turning on your computer, and lo and behold, just by accident, by chance, a new program appears on your desktop. It just got there and you don't know how. It somehow evolved overnight. Can this happen with your computer? Does this happen with mankind? No, no, no. DNA proves that there's a God because He has designed you, and the code that He uses is present in every cell of your body.

Now let me tell you something really fascinating, something called DNA phenotyping. Because of the advances in technology, phenotyping has come into existence in the last three or four years. In essence, phenotyping is taking a particle of someone's body, say a cell, then obtaining the DNA, the code, from that cell and drawing a sketch of the face. You can do that now. You can tell by a mere skin cell or hair follicle what someone looks like because the code has been cracked.

The first time this was done was in 2015 when a triple homicide took place in Columbia, South Carolina. Police collected DNA at the crime scene that they believed had been left by the perpetrator. They then "drew" a composite sketch of the man. The murderer was eventually caught because just one cell of the murderer was left at the crime scene, and phenotyping gave the authorities his face. It is just fascinating what you can do with DNA nowadays.

Now I want to pose a question for you. What would it be like if in every room you entered, every relationship you were involved in, every organization that you had influence in, maybe a business, a university, a home, what would it be like if you left trace evidence that would reveal the face of grace? In other words, would people know what grace looks like because you've been in their presence? After all, you are the product of the God of all grace. You've been born again by His power. You've been adopted into His family. You are to look like your Heavenly Father.

In this study of the face of grace, we're looking at how a graced person thinks. Later we'll see what a graced person says, then what a graced person sees with their eyes and hears with their ears. Right now we're looking at what a graced person thinks. In these first five chapters we are covering what is commonly called by theologians, The Doctrines of Grace. Those doctrines are Total Depravity, Unconditional Election, Limited Atonement, Irresistible Grace, and Perseverance of the Saints. I'm not using those words, those big fancy words. No. Instead, I'm telling you how God loves you even when you are unworthy. I'm showing you how He chooses you even when you don't choose Him. We've taken a look at how God in His love for you, and His favor and grace which is on you, seeks you even when you are not pursuing Him. That's what grace does.

Grace has a mind that understands the power of One to bring to life that which is dead. A lot of times in our relationships, somebody does something that ends the relationship. Maybe they say, "You know, I'm just tired of you. I don't want anything to do with you anymore," and they walk away from you. Many of us say, "Well, good riddance. I didn't want you anyway. You're nothing to me. Good-bye. Hasta la vista." Right? Well, grace doesn't do that.

Sometimes when people make choices in their lives, choices that by their very nature move them away from us, we say, "Well good luck to them. When they're ready, maybe I'll see them again." Grace doesn't do that. Grace chooses to pursue for the good that the pursuer can bring to the one pursued. Or, to put it another way:

A mind that thinks of others as,
Never Seeking, Always Pursued

I am always pursuing them in personal, relational ways.

Grace pursues even when nobody is seeking. In the doctrines of grace this is called "Effectual Grace" or "Irresistible Grace." Grace pursues and eventually wins. Consider this verse: "Even when we were dead in our trespasses, God made us alive with Christ by His grace." You'll find this in Ephesians 2:5 in your Bible. Notice the language. Even when we were *sick* in our trespasses... Right? No. Even when we were *weak* in our sins... Right? No. Even when we were *feeble*...? No. Even when we were *dead*, God made us alive with Christ by His grace.

I've been around dead people all my life. I either performed or attended seventy-five funerals last year, and probably a thousand in the course of my 35 years of ministry. When I was chaplain for the Tulsa Police Department, my job was to respond to every unexpected death in south Tulsa, whether it was a suicide, a homicide, or a traffic accident, and then notify the next of kin. Trust me, I know, dead people don't initiate anything. So, what does it mean for you to be dead in your trespasses? It means that in your estranged state, your sinful state of separation, you were dead to God, but then He sought you out by His grace.

The Bible says we love Him because He first loved us. (I John 4:19) I don't know if you've ever been to a church where on the bulletin, the theme of the church is written that goes something like this, "Making fully devoted followers of Christ. That's our mission." If you're part of that church, or if you're one of my pastor friends and that's the motto of your church, you've got zero condemnation from me. Do what the Spirit leads you to do. But I would say this, I'm not sure I would ever want to be a part of your church. There's a reason why. It's because if the emphasis is always on people being devoted to God, but there's no gospel presentation of *God being fully devoted to His people*, we'll never understand what grace truly means. Grace will merely be one of many "churchy" words that appears in worship songs or the pastor's sermon.

You may be reading this and you feel completely unworthy. You've never pursued God nor sought God. You haven't even thought about God. I'm here to tell you that God is the God of all grace, and He's pursuing you whether you've ever given thought to Him or not.

Let me give you a picture of this. In the Old Testament there's a book called Hosea and it's the story of Hosea and Gomer. It's an incredible story. Hosea was a prophet of God who lived eight hundred years before the birth of Christ. In a vision, God told Hosea to choose a prostitute and marry her. I can just imagine what Hosea did in terms of arguing with God. Are you kidding? A prostitute? However, the Lord had a plan that Hosea didn't know about. God said, "Do it Hosea, because I want to show my people a picture of My love. Israel is like an adulteress because they have left Me for another love. I want you to mirror My love for them by choosing a prostitute to marry." So, Hosea obeyed and did as God commanded.

The first principle of pursuing those who are not seeking goes like this. Grace picks the one not seeking a relationship. You're reading this and your wife is cold to you? Maybe your husband? Dead to you? Maybe you have a friend who hasn't talked to you in years; they're uninterested in you and you continually battle in your mind, "How do I respond to this person who wants no relationship with me?" Respond exactly the way Hosea responded, exactly the way God responded to Israel. Go after them. Go after the person who is not seeking relationship.

Here is the rationale that God gave to Hosea. "I will say to the one called 'Not my people,' 'You are My people.' " (Hosea 2:23) This is what God did to you. You weren't His and you weren't seeking Him. You were dead to Him and He came after you.

Grace will even pursue the one who is running from relationship. Let me tell you the story. Hosea found Gomer. He married her and took her out of her harlotry. She became his bride and gave birth to two children. You can read about this in Hosea, Chapter 1. Hosea poured out his affection on Gomer, but Gomer left him after just a few years and went back into prostitution. Now Hosea had the two kids, and his wife had gone back to her old ways. God came to Hosea and said, "Hosea, go after her again. Go seek her out. Go pursue her."

You see, grace pours out kindness on the one who ends a relationship. If this happened to you and me, we might say, "Look, fool me once, shame on you. Fool me twice, shame on me. I'm done with you." Our culture has taught us to think that way, so that's probably the way we would react. But that's not what God does to us, and we're to reflect his DNA.

God spoke to Hosea about why he was to pursue Gomer even when she was running. Consider this. Running looks different depending upon the situation. Sometimes the person who is in sin isn't the one running, it is you running from them. Either way, somebody is running. They're running. You're running. In both cases, grace pursues. "I will allure her to where she needs to be" (Hosea 2:14). I love that verse. It is through kindness. It is through grace. It is through pursuing the person who is unworthy that God and Hosea both brought Gomer (and Israel) back unto themselves.

I recently received a Facebook message, and the gentleman who sent it really encouraged me. He wrote, "Pastor, I've been coming to Emmanuel for a few weeks. I've never been before. My wife of many years has left me, and it was hard. But Pastor, I've been listening to the series on grace and how God comes after me and how I am to reflect His grace in the lives of others. And something amazing happened. When my wife left me it was hard, but over the last few weeks coming to Emmanuel, I've changed in my behavior toward my wife. I've been kind to her. I've not said a negative word. I've helped her get what she needs."

He went on to say, "Just the other day she said to me, 'Why are you so nice to me when I've done so many bad things against you?' And I told her, 'I'm learning that God treats me exactly the way I'm treating you.'" That is amazing.

Maybe you read that and you're saying, "I can't do that. I'm sorry. I just can't. Somebody gives up on me, I give up on them. Somebody treats me poorly, I just don't have it in me." Okay. No judgment. Let me propose something to you, though. "If you do not heal from what hurt you, you will bleed on people who did not cut you" (Unknown source). Until you recognize that healing has got to come to you internally, you'll never be able to pursue for their good the one who is running. And sometimes, the only way that healing comes to them is for them to see the power of the One in your life. Until you see the power of Him who is gracious to you, it will remain difficult for you to pursue those who are running from you. But when you understand who God is and what He's doing, then you get filled up with Him and His grace, and it just kind of flows out of you.

The Face of Grace

Let me illustrate: Your Father is called "the God of all grace" (I Peter 5:10). The principles that I'm talking about all describe who God is. This is His nature. This is who He is. He is the God of all grace, and you are called to "Grow in the grace and knowledge of Christ Jesus" (II Peter 3:18). My job is to help you grow in your understanding of grace and your knowledge of who Christ is to you, because God will "conform you into the image of His Son" (Romans 8:29) when you see who He is in your life.

Here's what I mean. Jesus is called our Great Physician. And as our Great Physician, one of the names He goes by is The Balm in Gilead (Jeremiah 8:22). You probably don't know what the Balm in Gilead is. To describe it for you, I've got to take you back to a story from the book of Genesis. There's a young man by the name of Joseph, and he has eleven brothers who really, really don't like him. In fact, they are jealous of Joseph. Joseph described to his family a fantastical dream of his older brothers bowing down to him as their ruler. The boys' father, Jacob (renamed Israel), gives to Joseph a beautiful coat of many colors. Joseph's brothers don't like hearing about the dream, nor do they like watching their father show favoritism to their younger brother, so they take out their anger on Joseph. They plot to kill him.

You can read about it in the book of Genesis. They take the coat off his back, they tear it up with a knife and pour animal blood on it, and they plan to take the coat back to their father and say to him, "The son whom you love is dead." Now they are contemplating exactly what to do with him. "Do we kill our brother?" One of them says, "No, no, no. Let's not kill him. Let's just send him away into slavery, to another country, we'll never see him again. But let's not have his blood on our hands."

So, the brothers of Joseph take this young brother of theirs and they sell him into slavery. It just so happened that as they were planning what to do with Joseph that a caravan from Gilead drove by on its way to Egypt. Here's how the Bible described this caravan: "The brothers saw a caravan of Ishmaelites coming *from Gilead*, with their camels bearing aromatic gum, and *balm*, and myrrh, on their way to bring them down to Egypt." (Genesis 37:25)

In the land of Gilead, which is just to the east of Israel, there were these trees that contained sap, a powerful medicinal sap that was extremely valuable in ancient days. People would come and they would collect the sap from the tree trunk. Sometimes they would cut the tree to accumulate the sap, and then ancient peoples would put this balm from the trees of Gilead on open wounds. If you'd been burned, the balm would heal you. If you'd been cut, the balm would seal up the cut. The balm from Gilead healed wounded folks.

Now put yourself in Joseph's shoes. The people closest to him have literally turned on him. They have cut him to the core. They have stabbed him in the back. They have wounded him. He is now tied up as a young man, heading to a country he's never been to, to live among people he does not know. His own family betrayed him; in fact, the last thing he heard from his brothers was a debate over whether they should kill him. How would you feel? Pretty rough, wouldn't you? Probably the way you feel when people close to you cut you, right?

Let me remind you of something. You are never on any journey in your life where you have been wounded but that Jesus Christ, the balm of Gilead, is right there with you in the caravan on your journey. He's on this journey with you and He's saying, "Your brothers may turn on you. Your sisters may wound you, but I'm with you. And I love you. I've pursued you. I'm with you to work good for you no matter how dark it seems. Trust me as we ride together to Egypt."

Do you know how the story ends? Joseph makes it to Egypt and experiences a series of trying circumstances. With God's help he endures, then he's eventually promoted to second-in-command in Egypt and placed in charge of all food distribution during a famine that extended across miles and countries. The purposes of God, by the way, are sometimes not seen very quickly. This whole story in Egypt unfolds over twenty-eight years. Joseph goes from favorite son, to slave, to second-in-command of food distribution, and his own brothers, their wives and their kids, even his dad have to come to Egypt begging for food. They don't even know he's still alive, but God keeps Joseph alive to save his family and ultimately the nation of Israel.

In Genesis Chapter 48, when Joseph reveals himself to his brothers that he had not seen in three decades, they fall at the feet of this powerful Egyptian who has the ability to kill them all, and Joseph says to his brothers, "Get up. Get up. Stand up. Don't be afraid. What you intended for evil, God meant for good." I would simply say to you, the only way you can ever heal from any relational wound is to realize the power of One in your life. He alone brings life where there is death.

There are four ways that I convey a heart of grace:

1. By not being concerned with what others think of me. When we're captivated by the grace of God, then we will never be concerned of what others think of us. The One who really counts in my life has already told us what He thinks. But you know, if you don't know that God thinks this way of you, then you're going to have a hard time conveying this same message to others.

2. By being careful not to view myself a victim. When I'm captivated by God's grace for me, I am careful never to portray myself as a victim. We live in a culture and in a world steeped in messages that suggest victimhood. But there are no victims in the realm of grace. When we understand that the God of all grace is on our side

and that He works all things for our good, the victim mentality fades away.

3. By being confident in who I am so I am lacking nothing. I am confident in who I am because I know who I am, and I will demand nothing from you because I am complete in Christ. When we understand that the God of all grace is the power of One, that He's the One who brings life to me in the midst of death, then whatever you can give me is temporary and it pales in comparison to what He has already given to me eternally.

4. By being captivated by God's grace so that I embody grace. And finally, I find myself so captivated, I just convey that grace naturally. It's not a command. No, no, no. I can't help it. Everywhere I am, my DNA just rubs off. It's who I am.

We made a video to share a couple's story which illustrates these principles. Here's their story. The couple came in just to share with me what God was doing. The husband sat there not saying much at all, but his eyes glistened while his wife shared. She said, "Wade, I left my husband a couple of years ago and I was gone for a year because I was tired. I was burned out, so I left him. I just walked out. For one year my husband never said an unkind word to me. For one year while I was gone, whatever I needed, he was there for me. I had surgery and he was there to be with me. When I asked for help to move out, he moved the furniture for me and never said an angry word. For twelve months! When I was running from him, he always pursued me, not for himself but for my good."

She began to sob and then said, "I really never knew what love was until that year." She said, "Pastor, for the last 18 months we've been reconciled. We're back together. We've renewed our vows. But I just want you to know that this message of grace that you're teaching, I've seen it. I've seen it! And it brought life to my dead soul."

You cannot in any form or fashion control people around you. That's not even in our textbook. The idea that we control people is foreign to the New Testament. You can't force somebody to stay with you. You can't by law keep people in relationship with you. No, no, no. Not only that, grace frees people to go wherever they choose. And by the way, if you've been divorced once, twice, three times, however many times, you're just as valuable in the Kingdom of God as the person who has been married for 35 years. Here's the truth I'm trying to get across: whenever anyone ends the relationship by their choice, you still treat them the way God treats you.

My wife shared with me recently, "Wade, you know I think part of the struggle that I had was that I grew up in a Baptist Church where it was all about performance, and I was told as a little GA (Girls in Action) girl that you do this and this and this. And then I became a teenage girl and I was a good little teenage Baptist girl, and I didn't drink or smoke or do all the stuff that others were doing. And so, I grew up in a church where really I was the perfect little Baptist girl, and grace didn't mean anything to me because everything God did for me, I felt I deserved."

I think she put her finger on something. I think churches that try to reach people who think they're deserving of whatever God gives, are churches that will wind up keeping people out when members see flaws in new attenders. But if you ever find a church, a spiritual home where there's grace, and you're a member, you'll let people ask questions. You'll allow people to run. You'll let people hurt. You'll even let people hurt you because you don't need anybody except the One who brings life to what was dead.

Chapter Four Discussion Questions

1. Especially in today's culture, how can we overcome the pull toward a "victim mentality" when we face misfortune?

2. In the story of Hosea and his adulterous wife, who do they each represent?

3. In which of your life circumstances are you like Hosea? like Gomer?

4. How can we live in such a way that we will leave a "trace of grace" wherever we go?

Chapter Five

"Never Finishing; Always Completed"

Philippians 1:6
"He who began a good work in you will carry it to completion."

I don't know how many of you like to travel, but I've been around the United States and I have also had the privilege of going to other countries. I have to say to you though, I have never seen a more beautiful landscape than Western Oklahoma. This week I drove about two and a half hours to Sentinel, Oklahoma for a funeral, and I took the back roads. I came back by way of Fairview on my way home. I think that living in Western Oklahoma we get used to the landscape, but if you haven't done so, you need to take a moment just to take a fresh look around.

I was talking recently with a woman from Fairview. She was in her 80s and she told me that legend says, a person climbed the Glass Mountains, looked around and said, "My, what a fair view." And right there in the valley, a town called Fairview was begun.

Garen and Eva Martens who live in Fairview have been coming to Emmanuel for several years. They and others make the drive of about 35 miles from Fairview every single Sunday. Garen wrote me an email several months ago, and he gave me permission to share a portion of it with you.

In his email he said, "Pastor, I came across my personal journal from December 2001 where I wrote these words, 'A new me has emerged, one who understands grace and God's acceptance of me without my works.' I was always incapable of meeting the expectations that I and others placed on me to seal my salvation. But since attending Emmanuel I've learned that because I was chosen by God to be His, it's His grace and nothing that I do, which gives me my security in Him. Oh sure. I want to obey Jesus and work in His kingdom, but that doesn't affect my salvation or God's favor of me. My obedience and service helps others to know Him and helps me to avoid the pitfalls of sin. I have learned since coming to Emmanuel that my security is in God's grace for me, and that has given me a peace and a contentment that I have never experienced before as a Christian. I am free because I now know God delights in me." Garen then asked in his email if I would teach a series of messages on the subject of grace.

A few weeks ago I received a Facebook message from a gentleman who had been attending Emmanuel for about four weeks. He wrote me and said, "Pastor Wade, you don't know me. I've never met you. About four months ago my wife of 12 years left me. I don't need to get into all the details, but God has given me tons of grace to get through everything that's happening. We are headed for divorce, but Jesus has allowed me to be kind to her despite the pain she has caused me and my children. Two days ago, my wife asked me, 'Why are you being so nice to me after all I've done to you?' I told her, 'Because Jesus is still kind to me after all I've done to Him.' Pastor Wade, I would not have been able to answer her question that way without coming to Emmanuel."

Grace changes people, and I want to convince you as we continue looking at this series called *The Face of Grace* that the grace of our Creator can change us.

When I was a young pastor, I was often unwisely critical of people in other denominations. I would sometimes say things about pastors from other churches that I shouldn't have said. I've grown up a little since then. I've gotten a little wiser and I've realized that I can learn spiritual truths from the very men I used to criticize. In fact, we have some Roman Catholics who are attending Emmanuel. Some of the best teaching that I've ever heard came from a priest of a local Catholic parish. I would often flip through the TV channels in the evening, and I have seen and heard the grace of God being taught by him. Amazing!

Maybe you haven't come from a church background, or maybe you've come from a different church background, like non- denominational or something other than Baptist which Emmanuel Enid is. I want you to know my heart. Most pastors and churches will say to you that they believe in grace, but my question for you and for them is, what is grace?

You see, even though all Christians will tell you they see the necessity of grace, some will say that to stay in the favor of God, to maintain the grace of God, you've got to earn it. You've got to do right. You've got to be good enough. Some denominations specify the things you must do. Oftentimes in a Baptist church it is simply to comply with whatever the preacher says. And so, what happens is grace is sung about, grace is even talked about, but in the end, people are measured by their performance. You're not as good as you ought to be, not as good as the leaders of the church are. *You should be* better, you *ought to be* better, you *can be* better, and so on.

We have looked at and studied the first four principles of grace:

1. "Never Worthy; Always Loved"
2. "Never Desiring; Always Chosen"
3. "Never Perfect; Always Embraced"
4. "Never Seeking, Always Pursued"

Now I want to show you that God's grace in your life will carry on to completion because even when you fail and you don't finish what you start, God will complete the work of grace He began in you. The fifth principle of grace is:

A mind that thinks,

Never Finishing; Always Completed

Philippians 1:6 is a verse worthy of our attention. In fact, I would encourage you to memorize it. "He, (that is, God), who began a good work in you, (that's the work of grace), He will carry it on to completion." Now that's a powerful verse. Let's look at the impact it can have on your life.

First, God's love for you is far more significant than your love for God. Now this is perhaps contrary to what you will often hear in Christian churches. In a lot of Christian churches, typically the speaker will make you the subject of discourse. You go to a small group and you are the emphasis. Discussion focuses on you: what you should do, what you ought to do, what you're not doing well enough. But look again at this verse, "He who began a good work in you." God is the subject. *He* is the theme of all Scripture. *He* is the initiator that began the work in you.

You might ask, "Why is this important?" Well, if you are used to being the subject, then God is the object and you try to get from Him all you can by what you do. That's not grace. That's works; specifically, your works and personal effort. If you think you're the subject and you've got to pull from God His favor, then it's always going to be about what you can do well enough. Usually the measuring rod that's used is how much you seek God in terms of personal commitment, so the onus is on you. If a person's love for God is always emphasized to the neglect of God's love for the person, or if you're challenged to be fully devoted to God while never learning that God is fully devoted to you, then you'll never fully comprehend the transforming power of God's love.

I tell married couples all the time that you will never keep your spouse faithful to you by law or by merit. If you really want to make your marriage affair-proof, you love without strings attached. You don't try to control what your spouse thinks or says or does. No! You love them where they are. You might say, "Pastor, I can't do that." Well, maybe the reason you can't yet is because God is just beginning the work of grace in you and you're on a journey. The good news is He will complete it, as you'll see in a moment.

Notice there's a second thing from this text. God initiates the work in you without any condition or merit from your end. Do you notice what Paul is saying in Philippians 1:6? It is God who began the good work of grace in you. You are the object. Notice that He began it. Now the million-dollar question is, why? Did He begin it because you drew it from Him? Did He say to you, "Hey, listen, I see you. You're fully devoted to Me. I see that your heart is where it needs to be, so I'm going to be kind to you. I'm going to be favorable to you. I'm going to be merciful to you." Is that what God did?

That's what some churches will make you think God does. But I have to say this to you; I've said it before and I'll say it again. I'm not embarrassed to admit to you that I don't think there's anything I've ever done in my life as a Christian, any good thing, whether it's going to the hospital to pray over someone sick, or visiting with a family when a loved one has died, or acting tenderly toward my wife (which I hope I can do all the time), I don't think there's anything I've ever done with one hundred percent pure motives for the good of the other person and for the glory of God. I can't think of one thing. But I'm not bothered by that because I understand that I don't draw love, grace, or favor from the heart of God by my being the best husband I can possibly be. He gives to me what I need because He has chosen to be gracious to me.

Let me show you. I Corinthians 4:7 says, "For who makes you different from anyone else? What do you have that you did not receive? And if you did receive it, why do you boast as though you did not?" Notice the first portion of this verse, who makes you different? The question is *who*, not what. You know if it were *what*, you might say, well, my skin color makes me different. Or you might say, well, it's my economic and social status that makes me different from other people. My education, that's what makes me different. That verse doesn't say *what* makes you different, but *who* makes you different.

It is God. In fact, the Bible calls Him the God of all grace and because He makes you different, why do you boast? You know what that means? Why do you turn your nose up at that homosexual? Why do you turn your back on that person who's been an adulteress? Why do you shake your head in disbelief at a person who was arrested for armed robbery or drug abuse and say, "I would never do that." Why? I'll tell you why. Perhaps it's because in your journey of life you don't yet understand who God is and what He's doing in you, because if you did, you'd never boast about why you are the way you are. You'd be humble about it.

My wife at age five was very young, but in her childlike understanding she knew that God loved her and she opened her heart to Christ. She was the paragon of virtue growing up. A member of First Baptist Church, Bartlesville OK, she was in the GAs (Girls in Action), a leader in the youth group, the person who set the standard for morality. Good for her! But does she have any room to boast? No! Who made her different? The God of all grace!

You know that sometimes in recovery, people who have struggled with alcoholism and drug addiction can sometimes come across as arrogant toward people who are still enslaved to addiction. You know why that is? Again, it may be that in their journey of life, they've not yet come to an understanding of who God is and how powerful His transforming grace is, because if we begin to understand who He is in our lives, we're not going to boast about anything. The struggling addict has nothing to boast about, because to be addicted is to be in bondage, powerless to break free. It is through God's power, God's grace and not one's own effort that addictions are overcome, so the recovering addict has nothing of his own to boast about – that is, nothing but God.

Ladies, when you were little, did you ever watch movies and imagine, daydream maybe, that you were the person in that movie? For example, did you ever watch Cinderella and ask yourself the question, "Why can't I be like Cinderella?"

In a way, you *are* like Cinderella! It may surprise you to realize that many classic children's movies that Hollywood made are built around a Biblical theme. For example, there's the story of a virtuous, courageous man who gives his life for his family or his country, like the Messiah who gave His life for you. Then there's the story of Cinderella, where a rich king is willing to lay aside everything in his kingdom to go after a common girl who has nothing to offer him or his kingdom. You are that Cinderella! Your bridegroom is the Messiah!

I almost hate to admit it, but a few weeks ago I watched the movie Kate and Leopold, an enchanting movie about time travel. Hugh Jackman, a great singer and actor, plays a prince in Belgium in the 19th century that is transported in time to the modern day. He arrives in New York where he meets a girl named Kate; they fall in love and she eventually goes back in time to marry her prince. This is more than a modern take on a classic movie script, this is your story!

The Scripture says, "For you know the grace of Our Lord Jesus Christ, that though He was rich, yet for your sake He became poor, so that you through His poverty might become rich." (II Corinthians 8:9) In other words, you are living an eternal story of love, and what God begins, He will carry to completion even when you fail at finishing your work.

If God began the work of grace in you and He chose to love you even when you were not worthy, if He chose to embrace you even though you are not perfect, and if He chose to pursue you even when you were running, He will complete that which He begins. That's grace!

This is the prayer of your Prince: "Father keep them in Your name, those whom you have given me" (John 17:6). He continues, "I have guarded them, and not one of them has been lost… I made known to them Your name, and I will continue to make it known, that the love with which You have loved Me may be in them" (John 17:12, 24).

I'm going to change tracks now and ask you a different question. What is your purpose in this life?

People ask me all the time, "Pastor, will you help me out? I've got to find purpose. I've got to know what it is that God wants of me. Do I marry this person? Do I take this job? Do I go to seminary? Do I become a missionary? Do I start a business? I've got to know the purpose of God for my life."

Here's how I answer. "I think you're barking up the wrong tree. God has already told you your purpose. It's found in John 17 where Jesus says to the Father, 'I've kept them. I've guarded them. I will continue to completion the work I've begun in them, that the love with which You've loved Me may be in them.' "

Never Finishing; Always Completed

In other words, that gentleman who wrote me just a few weeks ago is fulfilling the purpose of God for his life. He's loving his wife (who left him) the same way that Jesus loves him. Just like Garen Martens who wrote, "I have a new perspective in life," Garen is fulfilling the purpose of God. You see, grace completes what others cannot finish.

It may be that God has begun that work in you but you've taken some side trips. You've gone down paths that you wish you hadn't gone down. You've stumbled and fallen and you think to yourself, "I'm just not worthy." Maybe you've been divorced once, twice, three times. Maybe what's happened is you did something you never dreamed you would have done ten years ago, and it's like, "Where is God now?" I'll tell you where He is. He's in you, finishing the work which He started in you, and He will not quit until it's completed.

You say, "Pastor, when will it be completed?" It will be completed at life's end, for when you die and you awake in the resurrection, you'll no longer see in a mirror dimly or darkly as we do now. You'll see the One who became poor that you might be made rich, face to face. You'll fully comprehend what it means to love people the way He loves you. He has begun that work already in you, and for now He's simply continuing that work.

The good news for us is He never gives up on us. Ever! He won't ever give up because His purpose is for us to be Him to the people around us. You may not be there yet, and I'm not either, but you know what? I'm getting there and it has nothing to do with me. I love what Marge, my friend and expectant mother said, "Your waiting times are never wasted times." So, though you may be struggling right now and times may seem dark, He who began a good work of grace in you will carry it on to completion. That's the truth of God's Word, and He is always the subject of our conversations. You are the object of His affection.

Up to now we've considered the principles of grace, five altogether. Now we're going to move from the principles of grace to the practical aspects of grace, and I'm going to answer these questions: How does a person who thinks in terms of grace speak? What does a person *hear* who thinks in terms of grace? What does a person see who lives and operates by the principles of grace?

Chapter Five Discussion Questions

1. How would you answer the question, "What is your purpose?"
2. According to the principles of grace, what is our purpose, and why?
3. Why is it wrong to boast about overcoming difficulties in your life?
4. How do we live our lives so that God can complete His work in us?

Section II

A Mouth that Speaks

Chapter Six

"To People, Not *About* People"

Matthew 12:34

"For out of the abundance of the heart the mouth speaks."

I've been writing about how God is the God of all grace, and if we have come to faith in Him through the person and work of Jesus Christ, we will understand some things that are true about God because of His relationship with us.

First, we will never be worthy, but He always loves us. In fact, we will never really pursue Him with all our heart, but He is always dedicated to us. We will never be perfect, but He embraces us. He will finish the work that He started in us, because it's a work of grace and it happens independent of us. When we begin to understand who God is, how much He loves us, and the favor that He has for us, then we begin living like Him. We begin thinking like Him.

People around us are not perfect, but we find that we can love them anyway. Our closest relationships, family, friends, people at work, they may even at times turn away from us like we turned away from God, but we're not going to give up on them. We're going to pursue them the way God has pursued us. We're going to finish that work of grace for the good of the people we know, but not because there's anything in it for us. Oh no! It's just that God has saved us by His grace and now we're going to love people like He loves us. This is what Christianity is all about.

The Face of Grace

Now we've come to the second part of our series. This is where we look at how a graced person, one who thinks grace can measure how well they're thinking grace by the words they speak from their mouths. I want to begin by telling you about a scientific experiment. When you first hear about this experiment you may think to yourself it can't possibly be true. I felt it was a little far-fetched myself, but I did some investigating and discovered that this experiment actually has been replicated in a hundred different laboratories around the world. And it is in fact, true!

This experiment is about water, which we know is essential to all life. If you're an adult male, 55 to 65 per cent of your body consists of water. If you're a female, the percentage is slightly smaller. If you have a baby, its composition is seventy-five percent. We are made mostly of water.

There was a Japanese scientist who had a double PhD, one in chemistry and one in biology. His name was Dr. Masaru Emoto, and he performed some experiments and wrote about them in a book which became a number one best seller on the New York Times bestseller list, entitled *The Hidden Messages of Water*.

In his laboratory, Dr. Emoto took water and turned it into crystals. While turning the water into crystals through temperature variations in the laboratory, he also played a variety of spoken voices during the experimental process. He discovered that amazing things happened to the water. Crystals that were treated to positive speech, what we would call words of peace, words of love and encouragement, came out beautifully shaped with transparent colors. By contrast, water that was subjected to hate speech, evil speech, words like *I hate you, I want to kill you*, resulted in crystals that came out underdeveloped, cloudy in color, with no defined edges.

Some of the good and pleasant sounds that were played while water crystals were being formed included Mozart's symphony piped

To People, Not About People

in through loudspeakers. John Lennon's song Imagine was played. Love-themed words were spoken, including words from First Corinthians 13. Words of peace and comfort, then words of gratitude like *thank you* or *you're so good to me* were played, resulting in the formation of beautifully shaped and colorful crystals. It didn't matter what language was used. After all, Dr. Emoto was Japanese, and this experiment was performed one hundred times around the world!

The second experiment was then carried out. Instead of words of affirmation, hate-filled speech was played. Words like *I hate you, I want to kill you, you're no good to me*, and so on. Those water crystals had no defined boundaries, were not clear, and so on. You say, "Oh for crying out loud. That's crazy!" Well, it does look crazy and sound crazy, doesn't it?

Think about this for a moment, though. If you grew up in a home where you were subjected to comments made by a mom or dad that were cruel and hateful, you probably know that something became fractured inside you. My father was the son of an alcoholic, and my granddad didn't come to know the Lord until just a few months before his death. My dad has told some awful stories about growing up in a home where his dad was abusive, both verbally and emotionally. So, if you're the son or daughter of an alcoholic, perhaps you know from experience that Dr. Emoto may have been on to something.

But you don't have to believe the laboratory findings. You don't even need to have been fed a diet of derogatory speech like my dad was. All you have to do is look through the Word of God. Listen to what Jesus said, "For out of the abundance of the heart, the mouth speaks" (Matthew 12:34). Now, any time you come across the word *heart* in the Bible, you should think *mind*. Out of the abundance of the mind, out of how a mind thinks, the mouth speaks. You see, in the Bible the word *heart* means *mind*.

This is a good lesson for those of you young parents who have kids that go to Vacation Bible School or to Emmanuel Christian School. Let's say that one day they go to chapel and they come home saying, "Mom, Dad, I asked Jesus into my heart." Let me suggest that you hug them! Encourage them! Say all kinds of great things to celebrate that. But also take the opportunity to explain, "When you ask Jesus into your heart, what that means is the Lord Jesus comes to live in you and begins to dominate your mind. You'll find more and more, you'll think: 'What He wants is what I want. What He says is what I want to hear. The way He thinks is the way I'll begin to think. I want to have the mind of Christ.' That's what it means to ask Jesus into your heart. Your mind begins to think about Him."

Jesus would later say, "The things that come out of a person's mouth come from the heart" (Matthew 15:18). From the heart, or more clearly, the mind.

Moving now from the mind of grace and how we think, we come to the mouth of grace and how we speak. What all of us must understand as Christians is that we can think of our mouths as a type of thermometer. Just as a thermometer measures the atmosphere around us, so too your mouth is a measurement of your mind, showing others how you think. We can say we believe in grace. We can even sing about grace, but we must ask the question, "Does my mouth gauge accurately my thinking?"

In the Gospel of Luke, Chapter 18, Jesus opens with a parable about a Pharisee and a Publican (a tax collector). In Jesus' society, Pharisees were revered and feared while Publicans were despised and reviled. The gospel writer says: "Jesus told this parable to people who trusted in themselves that they were righteous, while viewing others with contempt" (Luke 18:9).

To People, Not About People

I want to focus in on just one word from this verse. Jesus told this parable to people who thought themselves righteous, but viewed others with contempt. Jesus didn't talk about people to other people. He talked to people about their problem. That's what grace does, because a graced person is uninterested in talking about others, and instead is fully devoted to talking to others. So, I want us to see that a mouth that talks *to* people and not *about* people is a mouth that has been touched by God's grace.

You say, "Pastor, you don't understand. I don't like conflict. I don't like talking to people about issues. I don't like talking to my friends about their problems. I don't like to talk to my kids about things they do that bother me. It's much easier for me to talk to those I love about other subjects, but not about any problems. In fact, Pastor, it's easier for me to talk with other people about the problems that my loved ones have."

I agree that it's easier to talk about personal conflicts to somebody other than the person you're in conflict with. But, the truth is that Jesus Christ never called us to live an easy life. No, no, no! There is a cost to discipleship. Living graciously isn't cheap or easy. It's valuable and it's hard. If you've never considered the importance of talking to people versus about people, maybe what's happened is you've never gotten used to thinking in terms of grace, for grace and true love are often more painful in the beginning than self-protection and conflict avoidance.

You say, "Pastor, are you kidding me?" No, not at all. If we claim to know Jesus Christ as our Lord and Savior, if He has saved us by His grace, this should be the fundamental principle of our speech, using words that affirm instead of words that tear down.

The Apostle Paul wrote to the church in Thessalonica, saying, "Admonish the idle, encourage the fainthearted, help the weak, be patient with all" (I Thessalonians 5:14). Do you want to know who my true friends are? They are those who will come to me and speak to me about any issue they have with me, not talking about me but talking to me, then being patient with me. You see, that's different from those who will talk to you trying to control you and fix you. The Bible never ever calls us to do that. That's not grace. That's legalism. That's manipulation. That's control.

But the Bible does call you to talk to people about the real issues and then to be patient with them. After that, if they run from you because they don't like what you said, hey, remember that you once ran from God and He pursued you. So, you know what? That's okay. You're going to pursue them even though they run. If they don't like you and they shake their fist in your face saying, "How dare you talk to me about that?" You know what? The One who really counts in life loves you no matter what, and He embraces you even if you're imperfect in the way you bring things up. So, you can be okay when others get upset with you because the One who counts embraces you when you're not perfect. Are you with me? This talking to people is the measure of grace in your mind. Talking about people rather than to people is called gossip, and it's a sin.

Have you ever wondered why churches are so full of people who gossip, why businesses are full of workers who gossip, why schools are full of students who gossip? The answer is simple. There's no grace present.

Let me show you the sin of gossip from Scripture, because it's possible you may have never noticed this before. There was a young pastor named Timothy who was pastoring a church and he needed some help, because the church was growing and there were many widows, women who had lost their husbands to death. Timothy writes to Paul and asks, "Paul, what do we do? Some of these widows

To People, Not About People

are really in need." Paul responds, "Timothy, elect some servants who can wait on tables to care for these widows, but be careful, Timothy. Make a distinguishing mark between widows. If a widow is under 60, she still has identity and purpose. She can marry again. You may not need to provide in terms of getting her food and so on. On the other hand, if they're over 60 and widows indeed, provide for them.

After giving these instructions, it's almost as if Paul is anticipating an objection from Timothy or someone else, because he says, "Wait a minute, why not younger widows? Why don't we give them what they need?" Paul answers his own question by saying this in I Timothy 5:13, "…because the young widows will learn to be idle if you give them everything, and they will go from house to house not merely being idle, but also as gossips and busybodies talking about things not proper to mention."

Now, from this one verse I want to point out two or three things about gossip. First, the source of gossip is a lack of identity. An older widow understands that pretty soon she's going to meet the Lord. She's matured. She has a secure sense of her identity and it's in Christ. But a younger widow may still be searching, still maturing in her faith and her identity and so on. So let her work, don't let her be idle because idleness will cause her problems. By the way, the little slogan, "Idleness is the devil's workshop" comes from this verse, I Timothy 5:13. A person who gossips from house to house about other people is a person who doesn't have any sense of personal identity.

When I was a younger pastor, I became well known across our convention for a couple of different reasons. Do you remember when the Internet first came out, and people could get on their computers and write things about other people through social media? I would read things written about me that simply weren't true. It bothered me,

The Face of Grace

and I wanted to get online and defend myself. I wanted to set the record straight. I chased fire after fire trying to put them out. Oh my!

Have I ever matured since then! You see, if anybody ever says anything about you but refuses to say it to you, that's gossip. It says much more about the person doing the talking than it does you. Remember that! There's no use in you chasing to put out fires because you can't fix the soul of a person. Only God can.

You might think, "I can't just sit idly by and do nothing. I've got to set the record straight!" Well, I would just remind you that the One who sets the record straight has already straightened your character. He's the God of all grace, and He's your identity. So, just relax. In the end, the truth will come out. To quote Charles Spurgeon, "Truth is like a lion. You can cage the lion for as long as you desire, but the moment the lion desires to get out, the cage will not hold him."

Notice there's a second thing about gossip. The sensation of gossip diminishes over time. It's fascinating that in I Timothy 5:13, Paul says to young Timothy, "These young widows, if you give them everything that they need, they're going to go from house to house and they will gossip and backbite." The word translated gossip in English is an interesting Greek word. It's translated tattler in the King James version. That's a word I haven't heard in a long, long time. You tattletale! That's the word.

Do you know what the word *gossip* means in the Greek? The verb means to bubble up, to get more fervent in the bubbling up. The idea is like taking a bubble bath. You put the water into the bathtub, and when you pour the solution into the water, the bubbles begin to come up, first slowly and then more and more and more. That's how it is with gossip.

The reason these young widows will go from house to house to house, more and more and more is because gossip is like a drug.

What used to satisfy doesn't anymore. A gossip will require more and more salacious information in order to talk about people, more and more juicy tidbits, because over time the sensation of gossip diminishes. You've got to do more to get the same gratification. Folks, that's not grace.

We all know gossips. We all know people who talk about people. We all know what gossip is. My challenge to you is to remember that as graced persons we are not to take part in it.

If you walk into a room and people are talking about somebody, here's an appropriate question: "Have you said this to the person you're talking about?" If they look at you and say, "Well, no. Why?" you just simply say, "Well, because it would seem to me that we should talk with:

A mouth that speaks,

To People, Not About People

---

because that is what Jesus did."

Third, the sorrow of gossip is that at its core, it's selfishness. You may not like conflict, so you may say, "I'm not going to talk to people." The problem with saying that is that you're loving yourself more than you are them. You may ask, "Well Pastor, do I really have to talk to people about their problems?" Of course not. "Love covers a multitude of sins" (I Peter 4:8).

Everybody's got problems, and God doesn't make you their referee for problems. But here's the rule of thumb. If you see a problem, you will never talk about it with other people until you talk to the person who has the problem. If you choose not to bring it up, that's great. That's your choice. You're covering it with love. Just don't talk about it to other people. That's grace.

Are you with me? I want to persuade you why the mind of grace always translates to *a mouth of grace by talking to people and not about people*. Talking to someone about a problem is the most valuable gift you can give them. A gracious God and gracious people are always about giving valuable gifts.

The Bible says "…words spoken to someone are like apples of gold" (Proverbs 25:11). We have a women's ministry at Emmanuel called Apples of Gold, and its title is based on this verse. That word apple in Proverbs is the translation of a Hebrew word which means jewelry. When you speak an apt word at the appropriate time, it's like giving to someone a piece of jewelry, a piece of gold wrapped in silver. That's so cool.

Recently I paid a home visit to a woman in our church who's been a member for many decades, at least for as long as I've been pastor here. I had a wonderful visit with her. She is dealing with an advanced stage of cancer, and while keeping her name anonymous out of respect, I want to tell you this story.

This lovely lady is an older widow and she told me, "You know, Pastor, my deceased husband and I never really had much money, but by God's grace we were so rich." As I left her house, I thought over her words, and I told the staff later, "You know what? She's exactly right. I had been in the presence of a very rich person because when I left that house, all the words she had spoken to me were words of encouragement, words of insight, words of wisdom, words of challenge. It was the greatest gift I had been given in a long time."

I want you to think about this. Our tongues are powerful, and we have the ability to mold and shape the character of the people around us. It's been seen in the laboratory, and Jesus Christ, the

To People, Not About People

Creator of the Universe has told us the same thing. Let's make our words like pieces of gold, jewelry gifts to other people. The Bible says that words spoken about someone, or gossip, are the equivalent of being stabbed by a sword. We're going to pick up on this theme later, but I finish these thoughts with a true story followed by a challenge from an ancient quote.

A few years ago, in fact it might now be two decades ago, a woman made an appointment and came to me saying, "Pastor, I just thought you ought to know there is a leader in Emmanuel who's having an affair on his wife."

I said, "Stop. Don't say another word. I want to ask you a question. Have you gone to this person?"

"Oh no, Pastor, I'm a woman. He's a man. I'd never go to him. And you're the pastor. I just thought you'd want to know about it."

"No, I don't. I want you to go to that person." "But I can't. I don't know how."

I said, "I'll tell you what. You have a husband, right?" "Yeah." "You told your husband?"

"Yeah." "So, with your husband, get an appointment, and you and your husband go talk to this man, and ask him. Then you can come talk to me about that man."

I never heard from that woman again until about six months later. I just happened to see her, so I stopped her and asked, "Did you ever make that appointment?"

And she said, "Oh Pastor, I didn't know if you'd want to know or not, but you won't believe what happened. My husband and I called him, asked to meet him at the mall, and we sat down, and we asked him if he was having an affair. And he immediately broke. Confessed his sin and asked for help. The last six months, my husband and I have been meeting with him and with his wife, and they have not only reconciled their marriage, they have renewed their vows and we've been a part of that." I said, "Well good for you! Good for you." To this day I do not know who that man was. Truth be told, there was no reason for me to know because the people who knew of a problem went to the person to talk with him about the problem.

The French philosopher, Jean Blewett, said in the 18th century, "The man who with the breath lent him by heaven..." I love that little phrase; your breath even right now is lent to you by God. You don't own it, for it was God that breathed life into man in the Beginning. "The man who with the breath lent him by heaven, speaks words that soil the whiteness of a life; is but murder, for death is given, as surely by the tongue as by the knife!"—Jean Blewett

Do you know the God of all grace? Have you come to faith in Jesus Christ? Then let me encourage you. Whether it's your marriage, your family, your kids, your church, or even your business, let the words that come out of your mouth reflect your mind of grace, because there's power in those words of yours. It's just like Dr. Emoto showed us and just like Jesus told us. Let's make sure that our mind of grace is connected to our mouth of grace, and we'll be like Jesus who refused to talk about people. He always talked to people.

To wrap this all up: if you have a word of encouragement, speak it to someone. If you have words of affection or love, say them. If there's a problem that arises with someone you love, decide whether or not you can cover it with love. If so, don't say a word about it to anyone else. If you really think that for the good of the person the problem needs to be addressed, then go to that person and speak to them. Be patient with them as the God of all grace pursues them.

Chapter Six Discussion Questions

1. "Out of the abundance of the heart the mouth speaks" (Matt. 12:34). What is the meaning of this verse?

2. Why does it seem easier to talk about people instead of to people?

3. When somebody is talking bad about you to others, is it God's will for us as persons of grace to "set the record straight"? Why or why not?

4. What is the "right" way to talk to somebody about their problem?

Chapter Seven

"Speaks Intentionally, Not Rashly"

Proverbs 12:18
"Rash words are like sword thrusts, but the tongue of the wise brings healing."

Recently, one of our church members told me he'd had lunch with a pastor friend. This pastor had taught a series on the subject of grace, and when the series was over, the church fired him. True story! I said, "That doesn't make sense."

He said, "Well, my friend told me that many churches don't like the message of grace, because otherwise how would you keep people in line? How do you make sure people come to a corporate worship service, or that they give to support missions? So, they fired him because they wanted a pastor who would keep the people in line through external pressure."

The theme of this teaching on the Face of Grace is that we will never be worthy of the grace of God or of His favor, but we are always loved. The idea that one day when we are worthy, God will on that day bless us, and until then we will suffer a lack of blessing because we're not worthy, is just foreign to the Biblical teaching of grace.

Everything we have from God is undeserved, but He loves us. We haven't even desired Him as fully as we might one day, yet He's chosen to be gracious to us. We also recognize that it's a work He has begun and will continue in us. We are simply the recipients of His favor. We'll never be perfect, but we are always embraced. Of course, we are all striving to be better people, a better husband, a better father, a better mother, a better friend, but we will never be where we want to be. Even so, God still embraces us.

We don't seek Him fully at all times. In fact, there are days when we want nothing to do with the Lord. We might not even want to think about Him. We're pretty upset, pretty selfish, pretty angry, but He still pursues us. We may not finish our lives as well as we once hoped or would have liked, but He always completes His work within us. These five principles are called the doctrines of grace: never worthy, always loved; never desiring, always chosen; never perfect, always embraced; never seeking, always pursued; and never finishing, always completed.

Instead of applying these terms: total depravity, unconditional election, limited atonement, irresistible grace, and perseverance of the saints, I've just given them fresh names. If you're a theologian, you know what I'm talking about. I've explained these five principles in modern terms.

Now having looked at how a mind of grace thinks, in other words, who God is to us as the God of all grace, and having been told to love other people as He has loved us, this means we're to be gracious people in a dark world. We're to think of others in the same way that God thinks of us. We're to hold those same thoughts regarding other people. You see how this totally transforms our view of this world. In fact, when we're thinking about people that we think need to change, the real change takes place in our minds when instead we think of others the way God thinks of us.

As a review, Scripture tells us that out of the abundance of the heart the mouth speaks (Matthew 12:34). If you were like I was growing up, you were given the King James Bible. Every time I came across the word *heart*, I thought it was a reference to something mysterious or mystical within a person, like the soul.

But that's not what the Bible means when the word *heart* is used. The word *heart* means *mind*. So when it says in Proverbs, "For as a person thinks in his heart, so is he" (Proverbs 23:7), you should just insert the word *mind* there because the ancients considered the heart to be the mind, the way a person thinks. Therefore, the way that you think about God, about yourself, and about others determines the way you will speak.

The mouth acts like a thermometer. What a thermometer is to the atmosphere, your mouth is to your mind. If you want to gauge whether or not your mind is thinking gracious thoughts, just take a listen to the words that flow from your mouth. So, in this section of the Face of Grace as we move from the mind to the mouth, I'm going to show you that a graced person has:

A mouth that,

Speaks Intentionally, Not Rashly

Recently a woman stopped me. She was in tears and upset because the previous day, her husband had spoken to her rashly. She had heard me teach about how a graced person speaks, but she was confused. Specifically, she misunderstood how what a person says is evidence of whether or not a person has been captivated by the grace of God. She said, "Pastor, I know my husband's been captivated by the grace of God, and yet he spoke rashly. So, I'm confused. Could you explain?"

I answered her. "All of us who've been saved by the grace of God are a work in progress. And just like when you begin to clean out your garage, you start that work. You will never in an instant have a clean garage, but you will work toward that."

The Face of Grace

So too, when God began His work of grace within us, we had a mouth that reflected a mind not yet captivated by grace. Changing how the mouth speaks requires a process that takes time. I find myself saying things rashly, saying things impetuously, popping off at the mouth. That doesn't mean I'm not saved. It just means the thermometer of my mouth is registering some heat (something wrong) going on in my mind. My grace mind is still in the process of being changed, and that is revealed in how my mouth speaks.

The Bible compares rash words to the thrust of a sword. In Proverbs 12:18 in the New American Standard Version, Solomon says these words, "There is one who speaks rashly like the thrust of a sword, but the tongue of the wise brings healing." Another translation puts it like this, "Rash words, impetuous words, are like sword thrusts."

Now when you see the phrase, *sword thrusts*, you probably think of the Olympics and the sport of fencing where two men or two women get into an arena and they joust with swords. But when Solomon wrote Proverbs, fencing had not even been introduced. A sword was the offensive weapon of choice for a warrior in Solomon's day. It's how you attacked. It's how you killed. It's how you defended yourself. So, when the Word says that rash words, impetuous words, popping off at the mouth is like a sword thrust, think technically of it more like you would a gun. The best way to translate this verse in modern language is this, "When you pop off, it's like waving a loaded gun in front of others."

Oklahomans who have been around guns all their lives understand gun safety. They know how to lock it up. They know how to protect it. They know how to carry it. They are not going to put a loaded gun anywhere in a house where a child can reach it, and nobody's going to brandish a gun unless it is absolutely needed. You may say, "Well, Pastor, what's your point?" My point is this. Why would we as Christians spend more time guarding our loaded weapons, our guns, than we would our mouths?

C. S. Lewis was a great theologian who lived in the 20th century, and he is still one of my favorites. I have some friends who are agnostic, who don't believe that you can know whether or not there is a God. Some of them don't even believe in God, which makes them full-blown atheists. And so, I will give them C.S. Lewis's book, *Mere Christianity*. A couple of them have come to faith in Christ through reading Lewis' intellectual presentation on why Christianity is not a crutch. It is life itself.

C.S. Lewis wrote in his book *Mere Christianity*, "The sins of the flesh are bad, but they are the least bad of all sins. All the worst pleasures are purely spiritual: the pleasure of putting others in the wrong, of bossing and patronizing, backbiting, and the pleasures of power and hatred." These are the sins that are spiritual, and boy, are they bad!

You know what the sins of the flesh are. Sexual immorality, drunkenness, drug addiction, pornography, adultery, you know, stuff like that. Believe it or not, they happen to be the *least bad* of all sins. All the worst pleasures are spiritual in nature. The pleasure of putting others in the wrong, of bossing and patronizing, backbiting, and the pleasures of power and hatred. By the way, have you ever wondered why when you go to the typical Baptist church, the preacher is often talking about the sins of the flesh? Why is it that we talk about the sins of the flesh, but we don't talk about the sins of the tongue, the spiritual sins?

C.S. Lewis wrote further, "For there are two things inside of me, competing with the human self which I must try to become. They are the animal self, and the diabolical self. The diabolical self is the worse of the two." The human self is created in the divine image, so we're all to be like Christ, right? The two things fighting against that,

The Face of Grace

C.S. Lewis said, are the animal self and the diabolical self. The diabolical self is the worse of the two. The animal self is what causes the sins of the flesh. The diabolical self causes the spiritual sins, the sins of self, he said.

"That's why a cold self-righteous prig who goes regularly to church may be far nearer to hell than a prostitute." C. S. Lewis wrote in *Mere Christianity*. I kind of like C.S. Lewis. What he says may be harsh, but I think he knows of what he speaks. You see, rash words are symptoms of a disease. That doesn't mean that a grace person can't at times use rash, impetuous words. Oh no, no, no! What it means is, it's contrary to our nature, so it's abnormal. It's not normal.

James wrote in James 3:9–11, "With our speech we bless our Lord and Father, and with it we curse people. From the same mouth come blessing and cursing. My brother, these things ought not to be so. Does a spring bring forth from the same opening fresh and salt water?" We know that James is writing to Christians because of that phrase, "my brother." And he writes, "These things ought not to be so. Does a spring bring forth from the same opening fresh and salt water?"

Those of you who have farmland might have a spring on it and you know whether or not that spring is fresh water. You drink from it and it is wonderfully refreshing. You'll never find saltwater in a freshwater spring. You might ask, well, wait a minute, are there salt springs? There are, in Salina, Oklahoma. Salina was one of the first cities built in Oklahoma and it was built around salt springs, thus giving the city its name.

What James is saying is this, "My brethren, if you know Jesus Christ, there should not be cursing coming out of your mouth along with blessings. It ought not be." Friends, you've been captivated by the grace of God, saved by His favor. Your mind is now His, therefore the thermometer of your mouth should reflect the temperature of grace.

Speaks Intentionally, Not Rashly

This means when rash words come out, and they're capable of coming out of any of our mouths, those of us who know Christ should pause for a moment and realize the problem is not the person we're shouting at. The problem is not the person we're cursing at. The problem is within ourselves, and our mouth is showing us there is a problem. We've lost our understanding of grace.

Rash words are really one's attempt at relieving internal personal pain. It's a little bit like coming home from buying groceries that include carbonated drinks, when one falls out of the sack. You pick it up, and unbeknownst to you, the carbonated soda is under pressure inside because it's been shaken. And so, when you open it later, it just spews out. That's a little bit like the words that come out of a mouth of a person who's full of pain.

Now, Jesus Christ can heal that pain. An understanding of His grace toward you is like a balm that comes from ancient Gilead that will heal any wound, heal any cut that this world gives us. But, if we're not looking to Him for our healing, to His grace in our souls for refreshment, then what eventually comes out of our mouths is just an indication that we have not yet applied that balm from Gilead into our soul.

Rash words are given specific descriptors in the Bible, and I want to show you some examples of rash words.

Proud words are rash words. In Daniel 4:28–35, King Nebuchadnezzar was standing on top of his palace in the land of Babylon. We know it as the land of Iraq today. The king says, "Oh look at all that I have obtained. Look at the work of my hands. I. I. I. I have done this all. I'm the most powerful. I'm the best. Everyone worships me." The word *I* is used a dozen times.

In that very hour, God came to Nebuchadnezzar and said, "Nebuchadnezzar, the speech from your mouth is proud speech from a proud heart, and I will not tolerate it." He lost everything he had that day, and he ended up eating grass like a cow. He went insane, and God used that brokenness in his life to ultimately bring him, I believe, to faith in God.

Proud words are evidence that a heart has never been captivated by God's grace. Anytime that I think I deserve something, I'm proud. All we have to do is turn on the radio and what we hear is, get what you deserve, get the service you deserve. Get this product. You deserve it. And so on.

Have you ever wondered why God healed ten lepers and only one came back and said thank you? You ever ask yourself that question? Ten were healed, cleansed of their leprosy. Nine left without a word to Jesus. One came back, fell to his feet and said, "Thank you." Why? Why just one? Did the other nine feel they deserved it? When we begin to understand that grace is favor to the undeserving, and we deserve nothing that God gives us, then we will begin to live a life of gratitude, not pride.

There are other kinds of rash words. Gossiping words are rash words. In the last chapter we looked at I Timothy 5:13, where Paul warned Timothy about the younger widows who might be idle and become gossips.

Gossiping words are words that are spoken *about* someone and not *to* someone. As Christians we want to speak to someone for their good. We're not going to talk about someone to other people that are not directly involved in the problem nor part of the solution. We want to go to the person who needs help. When the Spirit of God captivates us with His grace, He will give us a discomfort about using gossiping words.

Lying words are rash words. Read Psalm 109 to see what the Bible says about lying lips. You don't have to lie when you understand what God thinks of you. Oftentimes the reason we lie is because we want people to accept us. We want their favor. We want people to think highly of us, but all this changes once we begin to understand that the One who counts already thinks highly of us. He's the One who created us, the One to whom we will return, the One who will give us the gift of eternal life and a home forever. He died for us! So, if other people want even to kill us, what difference does that make? Since the One who created us loves us so much, we don't have to lie to people to get their favor or their acceptance.

Vulgar words are rash words. Ephesians 5:3-5 tells us that there must be no filthiness or silly talk or coarse jesting among saints. Now the following may sound sexist to some of you, but I assure you it is not. I've been a person who has defended the equality of women for decades, and some of my Baptist pastor friends have not liked it. I've always believed that leadership is based upon one's gifting and never one's gender. I believe that's supported in Scripture.

Here's my point about vulgar words. When I was a kid, vulgarities might have come from the mouth of a man, and people might have excused it, but you rarely ever heard it from the lips of a woman. That is not the case anymore. The vulgarity from both men and women today is almost unconscionable. So where is all this coming from? Remember, the mouth is nothing but a thermometer. It's coming from a mind that has never been captivated by God's grace.

Destructive words are rash words. From James 3:2–12, we will specifically see in a future chapter how the mouth, the tongue, is like a small rudder on a powerful ship. We'll also see it's a fire that can either cause damage or provide warmth. Our speech is extremely powerful.

Mischievous words are rash words. Psalm 10:7 says, "His mouth is full of curses and deceit and oppression; Under his tongue is mischief and wickedness." Mischievous words are words that are basically designed to disrupt people's lives. When God captivates you by His grace, mischievous words will bother us and we will choose to avoid them.

Backbiting words are rash words. Proverbs 25:23, "The north wind brings forth rain, and a backbiting tongue an angry countenance." We see that backbiting means saying words behind somebody's back in order to cut them down. We avoid these, too, because these are rash, hurtful words.

Flattering words are rash words. Psalm 5:8-9, "O Lord, lead me in your righteousness because of my foes. Make your way straight before me. There is nothing reliable in what they say; their inward part is destruction itself. Their throat is an open grave; they flatter with their tongue." We'll see in a later chapter when we explore this further that when a person speaks words of flattery, what they're actually doing is disingenuously using words in order to gain something in return from another person. And the Bible tells us that all the words of a flatterer cannot be trusted.

Now these are all descriptors of rash words, and the Bible warns us to guard our mouth the same as we would guard a loaded gun. We don't want to let these rash words come out from our mouths.

Intentional words come from a heart that has been touched by God's grace, because when you understand that your speech is just a reflection of how you think, then you're thinking about God and His grace for you. You'll be gracious to the people around you, and you're not going to allow yourself to explode verbally just because you're hurting on the inside.

There may be times when you're on Facebook and you just see somebody go on a rant. It's usually focused on somebody else, sometimes everybody else. The commenter is just spewing vulgarities and filth and anger and so on. Don't condemn, but don't respond to them. There's a good reason to restrain your comments. They don't yet see that the problem is coming from within. And the same holds true for you in your relationships. If you're married to someone, if you've got a boyfriend or girlfriend and they're constantly popping off to you, it's not you. Their mouth is demonstrating that their mind is messed up. This means that if you regularly make changes to yourself because somebody is rash toward you, or thoughtless, or popping off at you and angry with you, you're not helping them, you're enabling them.

In fact, my rule of thumb is simply this: if somebody ever goes off on me in haste and anger, telling me I must do something in order for them to get better or for circumstances to improve, I will refuse to do it. In fact, I'll probably do even more of that very thing that makes him upset. Why? Because that person has got to come to the place of understanding that dumping on me is a problem within them and not a problem with me.

Intentional words come from a heart that finds healing in God alone. In other words, when you're grappling with God over your pain and not just popping off like carbonated soda under pressure, then you're going to guard your mouth like you guard your gun. You're finding your healing from God.

Intentional words always have the good of the other person in focus. You're thinking about others. Have you ever been seated at a table visiting with friends, just talking when all of a sudden you stopped because you felt this pull. You pause, wait a moment and you think, I'm talking too much here. I need to back off. Have you ever felt that? You know, that may be the God of all grace just moving in your heart, reminding you of His love and acceptance of you. When you really understand and embrace His love and acceptance of you, you become more intentional about listening to your friends and finding ways to encourage them.

By the way, don't pull back because of what other people think of you. If you ever pull back because you fear other people are thinking you're talking too much, you're pulling back for the wrong reason. Pull back because you're brandishing a gun. Maybe you're talking about other people too much. Maybe you're talking about people in order to backbite them. Maybe you're talking about people because you want people to think well of you. Maybe you're talking about things that are focused on yourself, your life and your interests.

So maybe what you need to do is just guard your mouth like you guard your gun. Because if you're sitting at a table and other people are with you, you are there for them. They're not there for you. Think about questions that you can ask them. Find out what's going on in their lives. If they ask you a question, answer them. Answer them fully, deeply, richly. That's friendship. So, be real. My point is this. If you've ever felt, "Maybe I just need to pull back a tad," that's just the Lord working in you.

At this point you might be thinking, "Oh, my word, this is impossible. I can't do this. Who can control the tongue?" You're not the only one who has asked that question. James asked it in James 3. We will soon look at how the tongue can either be like a scalpel in the skilled hands of a surgeon, or a knife in the criminal hands of a thief. The tongue can be like a warm fire at a marshmallow roast among friends and family, or it can be like a fire started by an arsonist to burn down a building.

What's it going to be with us? I believe that the more we're captivated by the grace of God, the more our mouth reflects our mind, and a mind that is captivated by the grace of God will speak words of life that build up the hearer, like apples of gold in a setting of silver.

Chapter Seven Discussion Questions

1. Explain how the thermometer can be a good word picture depicting our mouth.

2. How do the "sword thrusts" from the mouth differ from the thermometer?

3. Is our culture making it easier or more difficult to speak words of grace? Name some influences.

4. Have you ever felt the nudge of the Spirit to "pull back" during conversation? If so, reflect on what God might be reminding you of, or telling you to guard against.

Chapter Eight

"That Builds, Not Destroys"

James 3:1-12

"From the same mouth come both blessing and cursing... these things ought not to be this way."

I was in my early twenties when I first started my ministry. I did some funerals for people who were born in the 1870's, and I think that is when my love for history began. Some pastors conduct funerals from a book, but I have always preferred the personal touch. I really like to get to know the person that I am honoring at a funeral, so I do some research ahead of time. In the process of researching the person being honored at the funeral, I have been fascinated by some of the things that I discovered took place over a hundred years ago.

As a result, I know a lot of stories from that historical era. For example, in 1888 some murders took place in London, England. Five women were brutally murdered. Do you know who was accused of committing those murders? Jack the Ripper. "Jack the Ripper" was never identified, but many believe he was a doctor by the name of John Williams because the murderer used a scalpel in his crimes. Now, this week I'm going to the doctor because I've got a little skin cancer on my neck, and the doctor is going to use a scalpel to remove it. Have you ever considered that a scalpel can be used to kill as well as to heal?

The Aggies at Texas A&M University have a bonfire every fall where thousands of people come from all over and celebrate the university. They have fun; it's literally a party before their big football game that weekend. Tragically, on November 18, 1999 the bonfire collapsed. Twelve people were killed and twenty-nine were seriously wounded. Have you considered the fact that fire can either bring warmth and a celebratory spirit, or it can bring death and turmoil?

So too, the tongue.

What you say in life, what comes out of your mouth can either build or destroy. It's like a scalpel in a surgeon's hand, or like a fire. Your words can do one of two things:

You can have a mouth that,
Builds People Up or Tears People Down

Let's take some time to look at the words that come out of our mouths.

We're in a series on the grace of God. I'm trying to show you and convince you that God is the God of all grace. What that means is He is gracious to you. He moves toward you with favor.

When I was growing up, I learned the doctrines of grace in theological terms. These five doctrines were taught by way of an acrostic spelled TULIP: Total depravity, Unconditional election, Limited atonement, Irresistible grace, Perseverance of the saints. Probably very few young people or even adults can comprehend those theological terms, so what I'm doing is I'm taking these same principles and putting them in modern language to show how we are regarded as children by our Heavenly Father.

First, we are never worthy, but He always loves us. That's the principle of grace. We don't seek Him, but He has chosen us. We will

That Builds, Not Destroys

never be perfect, but He warmly embraces us. That's the doctrine of atonement. We may not pursue Him as much as we would like, but He is always seeking us. And we may not finish as well as we might hope, but He, the God of all grace, will always complete the work that He has begun in us. He is that gracious. What I want to communicate is when we start to become completely captivated by our gracious God, when we understand who He is and how He relates to us, the first part of us that grace changes is our mouth.

How can you curse a person who is running from you, who doesn't want to be a friend to you, when that's exactly the way you acted toward God? Yet He loved you anyway. How can you say bitter things about people who aren't worthy and don't measure up, when you yourself are not worthy and don't measure up? But the Lord warmly embraces you.

When we start understanding who God is to us, the God of all grace, then we will start speaking grace to those around us and we will represent God to the world.

There is one nagging problem, though. Those of us who have come to faith in Jesus Christ still struggle with our tongue, don't we? What's going on?

I recently had a church member say, "You know, Pastor, I had a friend one time who came to faith in Christ. Then the next day he came to me and he said, 'I believe in Jesus, but when is He going to change my cursing?'" Well, it doesn't happen overnight, does it? We all can agree with that. How does it change? The way you speak changes when the God of all grace gets control of it, as your mind is captivated by His grace. Let me show you what I mean.

In Chapter 3:1–12, James begins by writing, "Let not many of you become teachers, my brethren, knowing that as such, we will incur a stricter judgment." A gentleman told me the following story and he gave me permission to share it with you. He grew up in a legalistic, fundamental church where the preacher always pressured them about the need to get saved today, because tomorrow you're in danger of going to hell. Everything was all about judgment and the wrath of God and works. For that preacher, this was the message of salvation. It was the characteristic message for an independent, fundamental church.

The man then said, "You know what, Wade? That was Emmanuel 40 years ago, because that's where I went to church." I said, "You're kidding." He said, "No," followed by, "I've been coming for the last couple of years listening to you. The concept of grace has revolutionized my life. But you know what? I'm so frustrated. It's like 40 years of my life have been wasted because Christianity to me was always looking forward to a heaven that was coming, and knowing that the earth would be destroyed by the wrath of God. But now you're telling me something different. You're telling me that I'm to bring a taste of heaven to earth right now, and that when people see me, they are to see the God of all grace." I replied, "That's exactly what I'm saying." He said, "I get it. I'm living now. I'm living life."

If you were like this gentleman, you probably heard a verse taught from the pulpit, and it sounded something like this: "Listen, don't any of you ever look to become teachers like I am, because if you do, you're going to incur stricter judgment." The preacher would then explain it this way: "Preachers are going to be judged more strictly at the Great White Throne Judgment. So, don't even try to teach."

My response is, that's not right. God has already judged us on the cross. So, what is this verse saying?

Any time you ever stand up before people on a stage and even attempt to teach, you had better have broad shoulders and a strong back, because you're going to be judged more than anyone else by your audience. They're going to judge the way you dress, the way you talk, even the way you look. People are going to judge whether or not what you say in public is what you live out in private. You will come under stricter judgment by people. That's what that verse means. So, I would just say to you, if you can do anything else other than teach, I would do it.

In Verse 2, James continues writing and he says this: "For we all stumble in many ways. If anyone does not stumble in what he says, he is a perfect man, able to bridle the whole body as well." Verse 3 continues: "Now, if we put the bits into the horses' mouths so that they will obey us, we direct their entire body as well."

Verse 4: "Look at the ships also, though they are so great and are driven by strong winds, are still directed by a very small rudder wherever the inclination of the pilot desires."

Keep in mind that James is writing this text before the invention of machines.

Verse 5: "So also the tongue is a small part of the body, and yet it boasts of great things. See how great a forest is set aflame by such a small fire." Verse 6: "And the tongue is a fire, the very world of iniquity; the tongue is set among our members as that which defiles the entire body, and sets on fire the course of our life, and is set on fire by hell itself."

Verse 7: "For every species of beast and birds, of reptiles and creatures of the sea, is tamed and has been tamed by the human race." Verse 8: "But no one can tame the tongue. It is a restless evil and full of deadly poison."

Verse 9: "With it, we bless our Lord and Father, and with it we curse men, who have been made in the likeness of God, our Father…" Verse 10: "…from the same mouth come both blessing and cursing. My brethren, these things ought not to be this way."

Verse 11: "Does a fountain send out from the same opening both fresh water and bitter water?"

The Face of Grace

Verse 12: "Can a fig tree, my brethren, produce olives or a vine produce figs? Nor can saltwater produce fresh."

Wow! What is this saying?

I want to issue all of us a challenge. James is saying your tongue has power. Dads, you cannot sit at the dinner table and say one word without power emanating from you. Moms. Kids. Business owners. Teachers. You cannot open your mouth without exhibiting a power that you may be completely unaware of.

The tongue has power to direct. Any time you speak, you are giving direction to lives around you. James describes it through the use of two-word pictures. First, he uses the horse's bit. Now, most people in Northwestern Oklahoma know what a horse's bridle bit is. It's the piece that fits in the mouth of the horse and is controlled by the rider. We get the phrase *chomping at the bit* from this text in James. You'll see a horse who is eager to go. He's chomping on the bit, but he doesn't go until the reins in the hand of the rider pull or loosen the bit. James is saying the bit is like your tongue, your words. Whatever is in control of your tongue is what releases it to speak. Not only that, whatever is controlling your tongue is also controlling how it speaks.

During my high school years, I was an athlete. I played quarterback on our high school football team, which means I was not only the star of the football team, I was regarded as the star of the school. My buddies and I got a lot of attention from the student body. On the other end of the spectrum, there was a young lady who was poor. All the kids in the school made fun of her. I didn't know her, but my football buddies joined in making fun of her. As we progressed through high school, during my junior year she became anorexic and suicidal. She was placed in a mental institution and it became the talk of the school.

That Builds, Not Destroys

When she got out, she began attending the church where my father pastored, and there she was saved and baptized. I became her friend and asked her about her story. She told me a lot of things about her background, but one thing stuck out to me. She said, "Wade. I want to thank you for never being mean to me. But your buddies, their words, they scarred me."

Dads, we have no clue. Business owners, you have no clue. Pastors, we have no clue. School students, you have no idea. The power of our words is like a bit in a horse's mouth. We are giving direction to people, directing them toward good or bad.

James also uses the illustration of a rudder. Those of you who've ever gone out on the lake in a sailboat know that the rudder is a small piece at the end of the boat that guides the direction of the boat. Our mouths are like that; they utter small words that wield tremendous power. James goes on and writes that the tongue has both the power to direct and the power to destroy.

This text says several things about the way people talk. He states in Verse 5 how small a fire it takes to set such a blaze in a great forest. You know what that means? That means just a word or two here or there, something we really pay no attention to, is like the scalpel in the hand of a murderer, or a fire that kills people…and we don't even know it.

James goes on and writes in Verse 6 that our words can be an ugly stain. The tongue is set among our members, staining our whole body. He writes in Verse 8 that our words can get out of control. Our words can be full of deadly poison. And then he writes in Verse 11 that our words can be like an unintentional toxin, like saltwater. Have you ever gotten a mouthful of saltwater? It is not pleasant, and it can kill you.

These are the characteristics of powerful words that come out of our mouths. But the point of this text is that *the tongue is a power that can only be controlled by a Higher Power.* This is the point. James says in verse 8 that no human being can tame the tongue.

That's straight from the Word of God. No human being can tame the tongue.

A couple of generations ago it was common practice for parents to wash their children's mouths out with soap when they were caught saying things they shouldn't. Perhaps many of you reading this had that experience. As much as parents knew the power of the mouth, and words spoken, and wanted to train their children to be careful, the truth is that unfortunately no man, no human being, no parent, and no amount of soap has the power to tame the tongue. There are only two who control the mouth, God and the enemy, the devil. That's it!

You see, your mouth is like the bit, your mouth is like the rudder. You've got a pilot in the boat guiding the rudder. You've got a rider on the horse controlling the bit. Ever heard the phrase, "Has the cat got your tongue?" The truth of the matter is we should be asking, "Has the devil got your tongue?" because either he has your tongue or the God of all grace has it. And what James is saying is this, when you come to know the God of all Grace, it shouldn't be that out of your mouth flows bitterness and poison and saltwater, because you've got somebody else holding the reins now.

Here's the way Jesus said it. "No one can enter a strong man's house unless he first binds the strong man, then indeed he may plunder the house" (Mark 3:27). This is a parable Jesus told, and the strong man's house by the way, represents you. The strong man is the devil, and his house is you. But the one stronger than the devil, the one who binds the strong man, is Jesus.

So, Jesus says in his parable of the strong man that He, Jesus will come into the house, and He will bind the strong man, the devil. And then He, Jesus will plunder his house. And if I continued reading the Gospel of Mark or the parallel passage in Matthew, what Jesus says is this: "I will take possession of what the strong man formerly had. He had hold of the reins of your mouth. And I'm going to take them from him. He was the pilot of your ship, guiding the rudder. I'm going to take the ship from him."

Maybe you're thinking, "This scares me a little bit because I know the God of all grace, but right now He's not in control of my mouth." By the way, it's not so much the words that you say, the fact that there are four-letter words that are culturally offensive, profane and so on. That changes across cultures and countries. Instead, it's the attitude behind the words.

My friend, it ought not be that the unworthy person in your life is one you curse, because you too were unworthy, and God delivered you. My friend, it ought not be that the person running from you is one whom you backbite about, because you were running from God and He pursued you. My friend, it ought not be that the imperfect person in your life who can never measure up is the one you turn your back on, because God has fully embraced the imperfect you.

Brother, sister, your friend may not be seeking you, but you know what? Why don't you just pursue and love your friend? Remember, that's what God has done for you. And you know, somebody might not have finished well in their relationship with you. But why don't you in grace, go ahead and complete what is unfinished, because that's what God does for you. My friend, your words should reflect the God who holds the reins of your life. The work of getting control of your mouth is up to God, and He's going to do it for you.

The Face of Grace

The question is this, do you recognize that it ought not be that your words reflect anything but grace to other people?

Dan O'Daniel is a cowboy pastor who writes poetry. He also understands horses, and this poem that he has written pertains to the breaking of the horse and how that relates to God pursuing us and putting a rein on our life. Here's Dan's poem:

> As I put him in the round pen, he had a wild look in his eye.
> His only thought to get shed of me and you could bet he was going to try.
> As I stepped out in the middle, he began to come unnerved.
> And when I raised my coiled rope, he whirled around and swirled.
> As he ran in a circle, the dust began to rise.
> And when he settled in a bit, I gave my big surprise.
> I made a loop in my rope and threw it across his back. He jumped and snorted and almost had a heart attack.
> As he ran in the circle, he worked up a sweat.
> He's about to give me one side and on that you can bet. Finally we came to join up. He stopped and walked to me.
> All the snort and fear was gone. A pleasant sight to see.
> He'd made his choice. He was going to trust in me.
> But that's not quite true. And that's what I want you to see.
> I had chosen him while he was in the herd.
> I roped and dragged him out before he was ever curr'ed.
> I think that's how it is between the Lord and us,
> He drags us to Himself and we make an awful fuss.
> He runs us in the round pen of life until that fateful day
> When we turn to trust in Him in our own clumsy way.

Then we say we chose him. But that's not quite true. You'd
> have never chosen Him if He hadn't chosen you And put
> you in his round pen and then under saddle,

And helped you through the buggers of life that you were
> bound to battle.

Then, before you know it, time has run its course And our
> dear Lord put a fine rein on you.

Kind of like a good ole usin' horse.

May we all understand that God loves us. He's pursued us. He's chosen us. We are His. And His grace is seen through our speech. May our mouths be a thermometer of the atmosphere of our minds. We cannot tame our tongue; only God can. We must ask ourselves, who has the reins of our life?

Chapter Eight Discussion Questions

1. In what circumstances/situations do you find yourself most likely to sin with your tongue?

2. "The work of getting your mouth under control is up to God." What then, is our role?

3. As a person of grace, how should you or I respond to those around us when they sin with their tongue?

Chapter Nine

"That Speaks Gently, Not Harshly"

Proverbs 15:1

"A gentle answer turns away wrath, but a harsh word stirs up anger."

In this book entitled *The Face of Grace*, I've been trying to show from Scripture who God is to each of us. I realize that we each might have a personal concept of God, but what the Bible says of Him is true and our concept of God may or may not be true. Who is God really?

He loves us even though we are unworthy. He pursues us even though we're not seeking Him. He embraces us even though we are not perfect. He finishes the work of grace He begins in us even if we fail to complete our own commitments to Him. He is the God of all grace.

If you ask the question, what about God's judgment? Isn't God holy and just? Where's His judgment for my mess-ups and my screw-ups and my sins? All of that is at the cross. He took care of judgment in His love for us through His only Son.

When we begin to understand the riches of God's grace for us, we begin to change from the inside out. I have a friend by the name of John Zens who puts it like this. "It is just as proper to say Jesus died to create a new humanity as it is Jesus died for my sins."

Remember the gentleman by the name of Doug who said to me, "Wade, I really feel like I've been cheated my entire life. I've gone to churches, fundamental, legalistic churches. And it was all about Jesus on the cross for my sins. And I'm going to die unless I repent. And it's all about heaven. And nothing else was discussed. It was about dying and going to heaven and Jesus dying for us."

He went on to say, "Listening to you, I realize I've been robbed for 40 years of my adult life. I've never seen that until I heard you speak on grace and how salvation is about my life now."

Jesus died to make Doug a new human being. Jesus died to make you and me new as well. And one of the ways He makes us new is by us contemplating in our minds who He is. That's when we begin to speak out of our mouths the truths of grace. The Bible says, "For out of the abundance of the heart," and remember that every time we see the word *heart* we should think *mind*, "the mouth speaks" (Matthew 12:34).

I wonder if you've ever heard somebody tell a joke and then say, "I really didn't mean that."? Oh no, no. They did mean it, because the mouth only speaks what the mind thinks. And what I want to show you is that people of grace, those who've been touched by the God of all grace, have:

A mouth that,
Speaks Gently, Not Harshly

Some of you are possibly thinking, "Oh! Please, not this again!" Perhaps you think this because like many families, you get up to go to church when you don't have to. It's really cold outside and you could stay home. You get dressed. Maybe your husband's driving. You're in the car, kids are in the backseat, and he's going too fast. So you say something to him harshly, like "Slow down. We've got kids in the back seat!" Your husband responds curtly in return, it escalates from there and before you know it, by the time you get to the church parking lot it's a full-blown fight. Then you come in and the pastor says,

That Speaks Gently, Not Harshly

"Grace people speak gently, not harshly." You find yourself thinking, "Why did I even come to church?"

I get it. All of us throughout our lives will struggle at times with speaking harshly to the people we love. I want to prove to you that not only is that not consistent with who you are and who God is making you become, it's also a lousy way to live. Listen, there is no reason to beat yourself up over this if yesterday, this morning, or this week you found yourself slipping into the pattern of being harsh with your words. Let me tell you why you don't have to beat yourself up.

Recently I went to Tulsa, Oklahoma to speak to a group of men who are discipled by a friend of mine named Gary Richardson. I've known Gary for over two decades. He's a great guy, an attorney who ran for governor twice here in Oklahoma.

Gary has a group of doctors, lawyers and professionals in Tulsa that meet in his home to just talk about the Lord and how the Lord is changing their lives. Periodically they'll invite me to come over and talk, and they'll ask questions afterward. I was there just the other night. During the three hours I was there, every single man in this group smoked at least one cigar. We were in a cigar room, and a couple of them smoked two or three apiece. Now I've nothing against smoking cigars. I've smoked maybe a couple or three in my life to bond with my son's friends and so on, but I don't regularly smoke cigars. Those of you who do smoke cigars know that you acquire a taste for them. Tolerance may be even a better word.

I have not developed that taste, and in that room with all this cigar smoke I got green in the gills. I was feeling sick, but I made it through. I drove the two hours home to Enid and though I made it back, I fought through nausea as I got in bed. The problem with that cigar smoke, however, was not what I endured that night before coming home. No. No. The problem occurred the following day going to work at the church building. As I was getting in my car, the cigar smell was still overwhelmingly on my clothes, in my skin, and even after I had showered, I could still smell it. The acrid cigar smoke had permeated not only my clothes but my body as well.

You may ask, "Wade, why are you telling us this?" I'll tell you why. Because before Jesus by His grace and love for you chose to take up residence within you, you had a mind that thought a certain way and a mouth that spoke a certain way. Call it the smoke of your former life if you will. Just because Jesus takes up residence in your life and you begin to experience His grace, it doesn't mean the residue of your old life does not linger and occasionally crop up in the most surprising ways.

So if you struggle with a harsh tongue and you struggle with your words, or you come across cold and you say cutting and cruel things, or denigrate people and maybe talk totally contrary to the way God treats you, it may be just those old cigar fumes on you. It's not who you are.

Are you with me? This is because God is in the process of changing you. So, let's look at the process He might use. Proverbs 15:1 is a verse worth remembering. "A gentle answer turns away wrath, but a harsh word stirs up anger."

How about this verse? Proverbs 25:15: "By forbearance a ruler may be persuaded, and a soft tongue breaks the bone." "By forbearance," and this word, *forbearance* means longsuffering. A "soft tongue," or a soft word, a gentle word is the same word used in Proverbs 15:1. In other words, "By longsuffering a ruler may be persuaded, and a gentle word breaks the bone." I'll show you what it means for a gentle word from your mouth to break the bone of one who is in authority, and what that little phrase *break the bone* means, but right now all I want you to see from these two verses is simply this: gracious people have gracious speech as a characteristic of their lives.

That Speaks Gently, Not Harshly

If you have ever been around people who are always harsh, condemning and cruel, cutting and denigrating and so on, when the words that come out of their mouths are almost abusive, there's one thing you might say of them. This is not a judgment, it's just an assessment. That continual pattern of behavior shows they've never tasted of God's grace or His favor. They've never experienced it, because the God of all grace changes the way you think. And when He changes the way you think, the way you talk changes also.

In fact, I can prove this to you pretty easily. In the Apostle Paul's epistles in the New Testament, he always wrote with a certain pattern of writing that he never violated. In the first half of his letters he always spoke of God's grace, the goodness and love of God for his people, and what He's accomplished for you and me. Then halfway through, Paul would make a transition and he would begin writing about what our behavior is to be as followers of Jesus, in light of our understanding of Jesus's grace toward us. If you ever teach your children what they should do and how they should behave before you show them how much you love them, they're bound to grow messed up. You'll get them as messed up as the church people and churches that always talk about what you should do and what your behavior should be, without telling you the good news of God's grace.

Paul always began with the grace of God, and you always knew when he made his transition in his letters because you'd come across the word *therefore*. Anytime you see the word therefore in the New Testament, you should always find out "what it's there for." The reason it's there is *for* you to remember what you've just read before you go on. Most times in Paul's letters, his "therefore" means "Therefore, in light of God's mercy, behave like this."

Ephesians is an example of how Paul writes like this. The first three chapters are all about God's grace. There's not one thing you'll ever read in there about what you're to do. It's all about who God is, who He is to you, what He's done for you, the riches of His glory and His grace. God in His mercy, even when you were dead in your trespasses and sins, He made you alive.

Then Paul comes to Ephesians 4:1, the halfway point of the epistle and he writes, "Therefore brethren." Look it up. It's true! Paraphrased, "Therefore, in light of God's mercies for you, I beg you to live your life consistent with your calling."

The English word that is used in translations, particularly the King James Version and others, "walk worthy of the vocation wherewith ye are called," is *worthy*. Live your life worthy of your calling. Those of you that grew up in a church that was all about performance and what you did for God, scored points for Him by coming to church on a snowy Sunday. You did the right thing, hoping that He would like you and possibly make sure you got sales that week at your job, and so on. Now when you see that word *worthy*, you think to yourself, "Because God is who He is, I should perform to get Him to bless me." No!

The word *worthy* comes from the Greek word *axios*, from which we get our English word *axiom*. Do you know what an axiom is? An axiom is a truth or a principle that is so self-evident that when you see it, you immediately understand it. Here's what Paul is saying, "Since God has been so merciful to you, live your life as an axiom of His calling of you." In other words, grace people should be gracious.

Isn't that cool? In other words, if you want to know why I should not speak harshly to my spouse, it's not in order to get my spouse to like me. That's what the world will tell you. No. no, no! The fundamental reason why Wade Burleson should speak gently and graciously, not harshly to Rachelle Burleson is because I want to live my life in the spirit of the "axiom," consistent with God's calling of

That Speaks Gently, Not Harshly

me. And if God doesn't treat me harshly, then why would I ever treat my wife in a manner different than He treats me. Make sense?

Let me show you also how gracious speech, which is to characterize my life, is a corrective for angry people. That's what Proverbs 15:1a says, "A gentle answer turns away wrath." You know what a corrective is, don't you? I injured my back recently and I needed some corrective measures. One of our church members brought over a machine for my wife to use on me, and it gave me shock treatments in my back. I was getting some corrective measures for a crooked back.

A person who is angry and furious and talks harshly is "out of alignment" so to speak, and some correction is needed. You know what the best correction is? Proverbs 15:1a, "A gentle answer turns away wrath." That's the last thing we see offered by the world around us. In this world and in the politics we see on television all the time, you answer shout for shout, yell for yell, curse for curse, fury for fury, anger for anger. If I'll just talk louder at the hearing, then the other people who are talking loudly won't be able to be heard. This is the way of the world.

In fact, we don't have to look at politics, we just have to look inside the home. Here we have a spouse who says something very harshly, or at least we think they do because communication, remember, is a two-way street made up of what someone intends and what another hears. And if you're always going through life convinced that what you've heard is the truth, but without ever asking the speaker what they intended, then you know what? God will break you of that selfishness because grace always asks, "What did you intend?" versus declaring what I thought I heard.

So maybe the person is harsh, the one you love. What do you do? Do you just "see them and raise it by one"? If so, it just grows harsher and harsher as it escalates. Well, yeah, you might say it could be that's the way we grew up. That's what we learned, so that became our pattern. That doesn't mean it's *God's* pattern, and it's not His plan for people of grace.

When we read a verse like this, "a gentle answer turns away wrath," we're confused, because the only way we've ever known how to deal with wrath...which by the way, in Hebrew is just a three letter word *rak*, R-A-K, which means fury...the only way we've ever known how to deal with fury, if we couldn't run or hide, is with fury in return. You fight fire with fire, right? But the wisdom of God says no, "a gentle tongue can break a bone" (Proverbs 25:15).

What does *break a bone* mean here? In that verse in Proverbs 25 we're to see one in authority, a boss, somebody bigger than you in power or muscles or whatever, and the Bible is saying contrary to what the world teaches us, a gentle, gracious word will break a hard person. "Break a bone" in the Latin Vulgate is a reference to "hardness." That's amazing. You may have never tried it, but I would encourage you to because it's the wisdom of God. A hard person is broken by a gentle word.

When I was a kid around nine or ten years old, I was bullied by a guy who was two years older than me. Between the ages of 10 and 12 you get growth spurts among boys, and this guy was a lot bigger than me. He had a lot of muscles, and at every recess in elementary school he would chase me. Weeks went by with him chasing me every single day. It scared me to death; I really thought I was going to die. I was fast though, and he never did catch me. I think that's one of the reasons why even today in my late 50's, I really have a heart for women who've been abused, or for children who've been abused because I understand the feelings of being abused by someone bigger, someone with the ability to intimidate and overpower somebody more vulnerable.

That Speaks Gently, Not Harshly

You know how that abuse ended? One day I stopped running. I sought some counsel from my father, and I decided to stop running. The next time the bully came after me, I didn't turn around and run away; I stood my ground instead. And he stopped right in front of me. Sure, I was scared, but very softly I said, "Look. I don't want to fight you. I don't want to run. I know that you can beat me up. You're bigger than I am. I just want to know why you're chasing me."

I'll never forget it. This big old bully looked me in the eye. He stepped back, silently turned around, and never chased me again. You might say, "Pastor, but wouldn't it have worked too if you had just punched him out?" No, I don't think so. I think I would have been beaten to a pulp.

I will say this. The advice that I give to any woman who is being abused physically is to get out of the house. You call the police, and then you go visit your husband in jail. He's suffered the indignity of being put behind bars, and it's then that you are gentle with him. You speak words of grace and gentleness. We must put a stop to the bullying, I know, but what I'm saying is the Bible calls you to speak gently to those who are harsh. Why? Angry speech is never about the person it's directed at. Ever. This is one of the big problems that we have, we think when people are angry, they are justified for being so. No. There is no justification! Maybe in them something is going on, because harsh and angry speech is saying something about them, not about you.

The Bible says, "A fool gives full vent to his anger, but a wise man keeps himself under control" (Proverbs 29:11). We are called by God to be gracious with all our words. So, if we speak harshly, we're just speaking in a way that is inconsistent with who He's making us to be.

I've already touched on this, but it's worth repeating. A life of gracious speech is a continuum for God's people. Just because you come to know Christ doesn't mean you are delivered from your harsh speech forever. No, no, no. It's a continuum, a flow of time.

Your gracious speech today is connected to your past, your present, and your future because God connects all three. You say you don't understand. Well, if you really want to know how to get control of your harsh speech so that you stop it, and your mouth begins to reflect your mind of grace so that you speak gracious words, you've got to keep thinking of the love God showed for you at the cross.

Let me explain with this quote from *The Cross and Criticism* by Alfred Poier: "In light of God's judgment and justification of me at the cross of Christ I can begin to discover how to deal with any and all criticisms. No one can criticize me more than the cross already has, and the most devastating criticism turns out to be my finest mercy."

Do you know what He's saying? Let me just paraphrase it. All of us have really messed up in life. We've done things we shouldn't have done. We haven't fulfilled expectations that others have had on us. Even our greatest expertise falls short. We've all messed up. The true criticism of our life is dealt with at the cross, because everything that we've done wrong as a father, as a mother, as a husband, as a wife, as a friend, as a follower of Jesus, God dealt with at the cross. It's done. It's finished. It's gone. It's taken away from us. The cross, the finishing ground for true and just criticism of our lives, has taken away the criticism. This means that when you believe what I just read...

"If you know yourself to have been crucified with Christ, then you can respond to any criticism, even mistaken or hostile criticism, without bitterness, defensiveness, or blame shifting" (Final part of Poier's quote).

If you really know that you have been crucified with Christ, then your response to any criticism, even mistaken or hostile criticism can be received without bitterness, defensiveness, or blame shifting. In other words, someone comes against you and they are furious. They

That Speaks Gently, Not Harshly

are angry. Maybe you didn't do what you said you would do. You didn't fulfill your promise and they are furious. A gentle answer from you in that situation turns away wrath. A soft tone can break the bone of a hard person, even one in authority.

You might say or think, "I don't have it in me." Yes, you do, in fact, all believers do because Christ calls us to depend on Him and give a gentle answer instead of defensiveness.

When you begin to understand that He's already dealt with whatever criticism is true in your life, then you depend on Him and who He says you are. The need to defend yourself diminishes. You can be longsuffering. Then, when you respond to the furious one, the angry one, the hardened one, be gracious because Christ calls you to craft your words in such a way that you build up those who are around you.

This is exactly what the God of all Grace is doing. He's crafting everything in your life to build you up to become the person He has created you to be, and He will finish the work that He's begun. Now in light of that, you can craft your words in the same way.

I'll challenge you with another verse: "Let no unwholesome talk proceed out of your mouth, but only such as is good for edification according to the need of the moment, so that it will give grace to those who hear." Ephesians 4:29.

Man! That's powerful. The Greek word translated *unwholesome* in the text, "do not let any unwholesome word proceed out of your mouth" is the word from which we get our word rotten or *foul*. In fact, it has the idea as used in the New Testament of something living, that has died and begun to decay. It's corrupt. It's foul. It stinks. It's rotten. Don't let that kind of unwholesome speech come out of your mouth. It's not who you are.

Craft your words as you think upon who God is to you so that they edify those who are around you. This word *edification* means to build up.

The Face of Grace

By the way, this verse Ephesians 4:29 that says (paraphrased) to not let any unwholesome word proceed out of your mouth, but only those grace-filled words which edify perfectly for the right moment, is recorded just 28 verses after Paul encouraged us to live our lives consistent with our calling of grace. (Ephesians 4:1) In other words, Christ calls us because of His grace to be a people of grace who give words of grace to even the angry people around us. Wow!

So, here's the way this works. Let's use our pastors as an example. It's Sunday and it's been a long day. We've all been up early. We work hard on a Sunday and then we go home. We have to fill out an MSR, a Ministry Summary Report, that outlines our entire ministry every day of the previous week, and we turn it in before midnight on Sunday. Sunday! Sunday's a workday for pastors. Let's say we're home, it's late, the house is unkempt, and the kids are crying. We're tired, and when our wife walks into the room we say something harsh or cruel. Can that happen? Of course. What's that all about? It's the smoke of the old life that died at the cross. No one is saying that the old life will not have lingering effects in our new life. Just like the way that cigar smoke still stayed with me, even though I was no longer in it.

Unbelievable.

What it does mean is this. When you speak a harsh word that is inconsistent with your character and who you are, and particularly inconsistent with who God is to you, you just simply say, "Listen, I'm so sorry. You remember when I barked, 'Where's dinner? Why isn't the house picked up? What have you been doing all day?' I was wrong. Will you forgive me? That's my old life. Just pray for me as I contemplate who God is to me and what He's doing in my life, because I really want to craft my words in such a way that, Sweetheart, when you listen to what I say or you see me live, I want it to be an axiom, a clear and present example of who the God of all Grace is to me. I want to be Him to you, and I wasn't. Will you forgive me?"

In order for this to happen, grace has got to be real. Not just a song, not just a word, not just a sermon. It's got to be real. May it be real in each of us.

Chapter Nine Discussion Questions

1. Is there a person in your life that regularly speaks harshly? How do you normally react inside when you hear those comments?
2. What is different about asking, "What did you intend (by what you said)" when a harsh comment has been made?
3. Name a couple of scriptures (memorize them!) from this chapter that can remind you to speak words of grace when you find yourself in a tense situation.

Chapter Ten

"That Speaks For Others' Good, Not My Gain"

Psalm 5:8-10

"O Lord, lead me ... make Your way straight before me."

If you ever refer to the entire Book of Psalms, it's always in the plural, The Psalms, but if you refer to only one chapter of the book, it is always singular, as in Psalm (followed by the number). For example, let's look at Psalm 5.

We've been asking and trying to give some answers to the question, "Who is God to us?" Scripture tells us that He is the God of all grace, so what does that mean? What does grace look like? What is the face of grace?

Our worthiness does not factor into God's equation. Even though we are not as lovable as we would like to be, He loves us. Even though we may not be desiring Him as we once did or one day will, He's choosing us. Even though we're not perfect and never will be, He warmly embraces us. And even though there are those days when we're not seeking Him, He always pursues us. He will finish what He started even if we don't complete what we commit to. That's grace.

What we find is that God in His love for us will eventually bring us to a place where we truly understand who He is to us. It may be that we wind up flat on our back looking up, with God warmly saying, "Listen, I've always been here for you. I love you. I am in your court." That's how good and gracious God is.

Now you and I, if we have come to faith in Christ, are to be emblem bearers of our God. We were made in His image, and remember, He's the God of all grace, so grace should be natural for people. That's the way the world should be because all of us are made in His image. Tragically, sin has messed up that image. It happened in the garden and it has been happening ever since. Redemption is the God of all grace reaching down and delivering His people, to turn them back into image bearers of Himself. All that means is that when people look at us, they ought to see the God of all grace.

The principles of grace should affect every relationship we have every day of our life, and to show you how this works I want to share with you the testimony of two people, a husband and his wife. The wife got burned out in their marriage. She calls it a breakdown and she left her husband, but he showed grace to this woman who left him. Here's what she says about seeing the grace of God in her husband.

Wife: "We got married kind of abruptly, almost 15 years ago. One day we were sitting together and talking and I said, 'Hey, when are we going to go do something, purely as friends?' Well, little did I know I would be his fiancée by the end of that first date. But we'd known each other casually for a long, long time but that was our first date. We were married a week later. My daughter was living with us and I was in constant turmoil because of that. She was very needy. I found myself putting her first rather than my marriage. I was also working in a very stressful job, and I'd been thinking for some time that things weren't right. Later while driving in the car together, I said something, then he said something, and a full-blown argument happened. Then I said, 'I'm done.' You know, I just snapped at that moment. I just snapped. I just couldn't do it anymore.

"I first said I'm done, it was just I'm done. I mean, I just needed to get out of it. I just couldn't make it work. I was just bummed out. I now call it a breakdown. It was just too much. I burned out on life and everything. So, we ended up selling our home and when it came time to move, he helped me move, you know. Go figure! He never was hateful about helping me move or anything."

Husband responds: "I just figured that it was over when she said that. But I was not going to throw any gas on the fire. I figured that we were through, but I still loved her. I still love her. I've loved her since the moment I asked her to marry me. And it didn't matter. I knew God still had everything under control."

Wife: "He was just there for me all the time, any time I needed him. He never once told me no, never once."

Husband: "I knew I still loved her, and I felt like she still loved me. But so many things had just caved in on her. She just couldn't handle it. I tried to help her and I tried to talk to her. No matter what I said or what I did, it just caved in on her anyway. And I didn't really know what to say."

Wife: "He stood by me the whole time. He loved me through it the whole time, and through him, I didn't realize this till later, God was using him to show me what grace was. And looking back at it now, it was just a miracle to me. It was just awesome that God did that. He did it for me through him. And we got back together about a year and a half ago. I moved back in with him, and ever since then, it's just been, it's been great.

"I look back and I see that God has brought me through so many difficult times, emotional things and such. But He is faithful. He's always there. Grace, I think, is just unconditional love and acceptance."

Through that couple's story, God is showing us how He calls us to be like Him to the people around us.

I get e-mails from people all over. There was one in my inbox recently from a pastor friend. In it he said, "Wade, I've been meaning to write you for a long time. I'm embarrassed. I even hate to write what I'm about to write, but I know of all the people in the world, you will accept me. I have struggled with same-sex attraction all my life. But now I've hurt my wife, I've hurt my church. I hope you can forgive me. I hope the Kingdom of Christ has not been damaged." Then he simply signed his name.

I immediately responded. I hadn't heard anything about it up to that time. I don't know if anything publicly ever went on. I don't know if he'd been arrested for solicitation. I had no details to go by, but here's what I said, "I love you. You're forgiven by me. I'm here for you. And by the way, I've got a whole long list of sins that I battle, I have battled, and I'll battle until the day I die. Why is the sin you're battling with any different than my sins? I want you to call me. I want to talk to you. I want to walk with you through whatever you're going through."

You might think, "Why are you telling us about this?" Well, because as I was writing I was thinking to myself about how God treats me, and I wanted to reflect this in how I treated this friend.

The way I responded to that pastor was a reflection of how I view God as revealed in Scripture and how He treats His kids. I tell you that because we're about to see another aspect of the *Face of Grace*. We're going to look at how God's kids have:

A mouth that,

Speaks for Others' Good, Not My Gain

You see, typically in evangelical churches when we condemn sin, we pick out the sins that we don't struggle with, things like homosexuality. We choose that as the example of an ungodly, heinous transgression, and how people need to repent of it, and so on. Why do we do that? Why especially, when the Bible says more about the mouth of God's children than it does about sins of the flesh? Are you with me?

In this text, I want to focus on the fight against the way we talk rather than pointing out sins in other people, because if God has saved us by His grace, it should be reflected by what we say.

Psalm 5:8-9 reads: "Oh, Lord, lead me in your righteousness because of my foes. Make Your way straight before me. There is nothing reliable in what they say; their inward part is destruction itself. Their throat is an open grave; they flatter with their tongue."

"There is nothing reliable in what they say." The they in that phrase are the enemies of God, the enemies of King David who is writing the song. "Their inward part is destruction itself. Their throat is an open grave. They flatter with their tongue."

Take a look at that first phrase of verse nine. "There is nothing reliable in what the unrighteous say." Now, when you first read that, don't you think that maybe the psalmist is talking about lying, that is, that the wicked are those that are liars? That's what I thought. But look at the last phrase of this verse. "They flatter with their tongue."

Going on to Verse 10, "Hold them guilty O God; by their own devices," referring back to their tongue, their flattery, their open throat, "let them fall. In the multitude of their transgressions thrust them out, for they are rebellious against You." I find it fascinating that in the Psalms when the wicked are described, it's the sins of the mouth that indict them, not the sins of the flesh.

Now, that doesn't mean that sins of the flesh and fighting them are not important. As I told my pastor friend, I'll help him to keep fighting. My point is this. Why do we hold people in judgment and condemnation for sins we don't struggle with, and yet we never think about the sins we commit with our own mouth?

So, speaking to myself, the contrast between the wicked and the righteous is seen in the mouth. Flattery is defined as excessive and insincere praise given especially, and here's the key phrase, to further one's own self-interests. The wicked flatter. The righteous do not. The people of grace who reflect the image of the God of all grace don't engage in flattery. Flattery is comprised of words of praise that are given disingenuously with the expectation of favors in return. In other words, if I were to flatter you, I am shaping and forming my words to excessively praise you or what you've done, and all for one purpose: I want something from you.

What is the difference between genuine praise and flattery? I think Dale Carnegie nails it when he says, "Flattery is from the teeth out. Appreciation or praise is from the heart out."

A little side note: if anyone ever praises you, the Bible says *love believes all things*. Believe that the person praising you is sincere and not wanting something from you. Don't go to motive. Just receive the praise. You see, flattery cannot be determined by the hearer. It can only be identified by the speaker.

Graced people are to avoid flattery. I am to avoid forming and shaping my words in order to get something from you. Why? Because flattery is harmful both to the speaker and to the subject who is being flattered. You may ask, how is it harmful? Here's what the scripture says. "A man that flatters his neighbor spreads a net for his feet" (Proverbs 29:5).

Spreads a net for whose feet? Is it the neighbor or is it the man who flatters? Well, I think it could be both. The context is probably the man who flatters. But the point is this. Any time flattery is present, a net is cast and people will get caught in it. This goes back to

That Speaks for Others' Good, Not My Gain

the ancient way of farmers hunting prey. They would spread nets, particularly to capture birds. The birds would land in the net to eat the seed that the farmer had cast in it. As they ate, their claws would get caught in the net and the trap would be sprung. This is precisely what flattery does. It springs a trap for the hearer and for the speaker. It's not reality or genuine. It's selfishness.

Flattery can be regarded as idolatry of the lips. Any time you flatter someone, excessively and insincerely praise them in order to get something from them in return, you are substituting that person for God. Have you ever thought of it that way? Philippians 4:19 says: "My God shall supply all your needs according to His riches in glory." But if you have to craft your words to get something from other people, you show that you're not depending on God.

Flattery will be absent from heaven and it should be absent from the body of Christ. I want to be a pastor and a friend who doesn't flatter. I want to be a part of a community of believers that doesn't practice flattery.

If your heart is full of joy and full of praise, maybe for Pastor Wade for a message that he delivers, never hesitate to share with Pastor Wade the praise that's in your heart. But remember this, do not expect anything in return from Pastor Wade. My heart is full of appreciation for Rachelle, my wife. My heart really, genuinely bubbles with joy for Rachelle, for who she is and what she does. And the expression of that praise is genuine.

If you praise your husband, your heart is full of praise, so offer it, but don't demand anything in return, even the return of words of praise. Expecting something in return reduces your words of praise to mere flattery. That's the heart of a person who's never tasted of a gracious God. I'll put it this way. Maybe we've tasted of a gracious God, but there is an idol sitting on the shelf of our heart that has taken the place of our gracious God. He will eventually knock the idol away. My point is this. You'll know that your dependence is upon the grace of God by whether or not you abstain from flattery.

The Bible is rich with admonishment against flattery. We see in Psalm 12:3, "The Lord shall cut off all flattering lips and the tongue that speaks proud things." In the Old Testament, the phrase cut off simply refers to judgment. It's a description of the wicked who will be judged by God. The wicked are those that manipulate through flattery.

Also in I Thessalonians 2:5, Paul says, "For neither at any time did we use flattering words when we were with you in Thessalonica. Not one time." I wish I was capable of saying that. I don't know that I could, but Paul could. He said, "We've never flattered you." The writer of Proverbs says in Proverbs 20:19, "Keep no company with the one who flatters with his lips. Avoid it."

Lastly, I'll offer my favorite verse of all. Proverbs 28:23 says, "He that rebukes a man afterwards shall find more favor than he that flatters with the tongue." Think about this in your own experience. A true friend is someone who will come to you in love, who will point out a shortcoming: a weakness or insecurity, something that you're doing that might be endangering a relationship, maybe a personality or character flaw, a habit, whatever…and for your good, gently rebuke you, not because of their pain or anything they need to gain from you. Solely for your good. That's a gentle rebuke. The scripture says that the person who does that afterwards will find far more favor from God than the one who flatters.

In my own experience I've seen this to be true. When I think back, it's the people who took the risk, those who came to me to point things out and give a gentle, gracious rebuke for my good, they're the ones who are my friends because they were risking everything to come talk to me. That meant they needed nothing in return from me.

So, my challenge to you is to remember this. Grace avoids excessive and insincere praise in order to get something in return. Grace avoids that. Grace gives praise freely regardless of the reaction, and grace refrains from flattery because we need nothing from the people around us. We have it all from the God of all grace.

There's a flip side to flattery, and that is backbiting. Backbiting amounts to words of criticism that are given in an environment of secrecy. In fact, the Hebrew word that is translated *backbiting* into English comes from a root which means *to hide or to conceal*.

Let's say one day you were in your car driving home, then when you got out of your car you were robbed at gunpoint and your wallet was stolen. The robber is stealing something from you in broad daylight, in public. A reputation can be stolen in the same manner; it can be stolen publicly. All we have to do is look at politics today. People are saying all kinds of things about people on television that they view as opponents. Go to social media where people are saying all kinds of things about other people. That's public.

On the other hand, backbiting is taking a reputation from someone secretly. Backbiting is defined as malicious talk about someone who is not present there with you. It is being in a room and discussing and talking about a character flaw, a failure, or something demeaning in the life of a person who is not present in the room. You're doing it all with a motive to steal that person's reputation. Graced people avoid that.

You might ask, "What if it's true? I'm sitting in a room and we're just talking and visiting. We're all friends. And the subject comes up about what so-and-so did and we talk about it. Now, come on. It's true. They did that."

Yes, I know. That's how I excuse my backbiting as well. Be as it may, grace doesn't do that. Grace goes to the person who is present and offers a gentle rebuke. If a discussion is had without that person present, a grace person will refrain, because that's who God is to us. Do you think God is going around backbiting you? No. Then I don't need to go around backbiting against anybody else.

You know, even this week I was writing something. I have some folks who kind of proofread what I write, who offered some gentle correction, some gentle rebuke. And it was truly gently offered. I went back and looked at some of the edits and I thought to myself, Look at that, Wade. I didn't name a person, but I was crafting. I was crafting what I was writing in such a way that anybody who would read it would see a weakness in an unnamed person in order that I might be seen in a better light. That's backbiting. I took it out. It read so much better and there was so much more strength in the point of what I was writing.

When God fills us with His grace, when the God of all grace captivates our minds, we don't require anything from anybody else. We're going to speak and craft our words for the good of other people, not for our personal gain. And so, there are times when my heart is filled with praise and joy for someone I know or love. I will share that. But I need nothing in return. That's grace.

There are times when a gentle rebuke is needed, either one that I give or one that I receive. That's grace because we're not expecting anything in return. I want to say to my struggling friend right now, "Thank you for your transparency to me. Nobody knows who you are except me. Man, I love you. I will walk with you through your fight against your desires for homosexuality. Will you love me? Walk with me through my fight against the desire to backbite, flatter, and gossip?

That Speaks for Others' Good, Not My Gain

I'm of the opinion my sins that I fight against are as deadly as yours. He is a God of all grace. He will help us both."

Chapter Ten Discussion Questions

1. What is different about sins of the tongue, versus sins like drinking and sexual sin?
2. What is flattery, and why should people of grace avoid flattery?
3. As a person captivated by God's grace, what is the right way to offer praise?
4. How is backbiting different from criticism? When necessary, how should a graced person offer criticism?

Section III

Eyes That See

Chapter Eleven

"Eyes That See The Best In People"

Matthew 22:34-40
"You should love your neighbor as yourself."

Grace. We can sing about it. We can talk about it. We can hear the word used in conversation. But how can we understand a concept like "grace" that sounds so nebulous to the average Christian? Well, we are studying what grace *looks* like. The way that I know you is by your face, and you know me by my face. So, what is the face of grace? What does grace look like?

Up till now we have seen how the mind of grace thinks. Then we looked at how the mouth of grace speaks. Let's now turn our focus to the *eyes* of grace and see how a person who knows the God of all grace sees life around them.

Let's think about how you and I look at other people and what we see in them. Do we have eyes that see the best in people? People of grace should have:

Eyes that,

See the Best in People

Now, there may be occasions when that doesn't happen at all. If this is the case, then we've lost our connection to an understanding that we are to be people of grace. I want to compare this to how God looks at you and me, what He sees in us, and what He thinks about us.

Those of you who know me understand that I love history. I absolutely love it; in fact, I'd rather go to a museum than a movie. My favorite museum in the entire world is in London, England, with the Louvre in Paris coming in a close second. The museum in London is called Churchill's Bunker, and I love Churchill's Bunker because of the significance of what took place there. It's the actual bunker where during World War II, Winston Churchill, the leader of England made his home. Churchill is the person I credit for the Allies winning the war against the Nazis. During the war, Churchill had a body double who was paid to go out to public events and act as if he was Winston Churchill. In truth, Winston Churchill was underground, conducting operations for the war in his bunker.

I'm not old enough to remember it, but my father told me about the day when World War II ended. Dad was a young boy walking along South May Avenue in Oklahoma City, when suddenly all of the whistles at the nearby meat packing company began to blow and people began to honk their horns. The war was over.

On that same day, Winston Churchill stepped out of the bunker that would later bear his name, and the British government sealed it. It was not opened again until over forty years later when Margaret Thatcher, the Prime Minister of Great Britain ordered that it be opened. They opened it, and now you and I have the opportunity to go down into Churchill's wartime residence. We can see the actual cigar Churchill was smoking on the last day of the war still lying there in the ashtray. We can see everything untouched. It's as though you are reliving the war in that museum.

The only thing that has been changed is the newly remodeled entrance into the bunker. Some of Churchill's most famous quotes are

Eyes That See the Best in People

displayed all over the wall. As Rachelle and I were walking into the bunker ready to hand our tickets to the attendant, I came across a quote of Churchill's that I'd never seen before. It read: "We are all worms. But I do believe that I am."

We continued walking quickly because we were being pushed along in the line, but I kept thinking about what Churchill had said in that mysterious quote. Remember, it was the first time I'd ever heard it: "We are all worms. But I believe that I am." I thought, what did he mean by that?

When I was growing up in a church setting, I was hammered all the time with the fact that I was nothing but a worm. I was worthless. In fact, the classic hymn "Alas, and did my Savior Bleed" contains a stanza that basically questions how God could die for a worm such as I. So, I thought maybe that's what Churchill was referring to, maybe he grew up in a similar religious environment where he was told from a theological perspective, "You're nothing but a lowly worm."

With this in mind, I thought he might be saying to us, "Everybody is a worm. I believe I am," meaning, everybody else (whether they know it or not) is a worm, but Churchill knew for sure that he was. That's what I thought anyway, until I came walking out from the museum, and upon rereading the quote I realized that I had failed to read the last phrase. As I read the full quote of Winston Churchill, here's what he actually said. "We are all worms, but I do believe I am a glow-worm." Oh, my word. A glow-worm? That changed the entire meaning.

Do you know what a glow-worm is? Far from a common earthworm, a glow-worm is a very, very special worm. Many of you know them as fireflies, or lightning bugs, the insects that kids love to capture in jars on summer nights. In the Fifties there was a song sung by the Mills Brothers about a glow-worm. A glow-worm is someone or something that is really special or unique. So here's what Churchill was saying, "We are all worms, but I do believe I am special. I am a glow-worm."

Believe it or not, Winston Churchill's statement has relevance for us today. May I confess something to you? I have changed over the years as a pastor. I hope I've become a better husband and a better father. I think I have. But I *know* I've changed as a pastor. Let me tell you, the most significant way I've changed as a pastor is in terms of my theology. I used to think people were all worms and that I myself was nothing but a worm. A simple dirt worm. Worthless. That was my theology, but I have since come to believe what Churchill believed. There is something special about me, and there is something special about you, because the Creator of the universe gave His Son for us all. God didn't give Jeshua for common dirt worms, He gave His Son for glow-worms.

Do you and I see the best in ourselves and in others? In order to see the best in other people, we first have to have a right understanding of who we are. Do you and I see the best in our families, the best in our friends, the best in our neighbors, the best in the people around us? The best in our co-workers? Do we see what's best in them? To do so, first we would have to really see ourselves as God sees us.

Our opening passage in Matthew 22 says that the religious leaders of Jesus' day were trying to trap Him. They were testing Him because He had silenced them, basically telling them, "You're not teaching truth. Be quiet. Let Me tell you how it is." The Scripture then tells us beginning in verse 34, that they were upset because He had silenced them. Matthew 22:34-35 reads: "But when the Pharisees heard that Jesus had silenced the Sadducees, they gathered themselves together. 35One of them, a lawyer, asked Him a question, testing Him."

Eyes That See the Best in People

We need to remember that lawyers back then were not like the lawyers of today. This lawyer of the Pharisees was one that knew the Law of the Old Testament. He was an expert in Genesis, Exodus, Leviticus, Numbers, and Deuteronomy. He came to Jesus to question Him and he said this, "Teacher, which is the greatest commandment in the Law?"

Jesus responded to him saying, [37]"You shall love the Lord, your God with all your heart and with all your soul and with all your mind. [38]This is the great and foremost commandment." He continued, [39]"The second is like it, you shall love your neighbor as yourself. [40]On these two commandments depend the whole Law and the Prophets."

All the Law and all the Prophets hang or are dependent on these two commandments: Love the Lord your God, and love your neighbor as yourself.

I'm going to show us something about ourselves and about the people around us from this passage. The only way that we will ever love others is to truly love ourselves correctly. In fact, I would propose to you if we're struggling to love other people, deep down the problem is an incorrect love for ourselves.

Read again what the Teacher said in verse 39, "Love your neighbor as yourself."

You might think, "So, wait a minute. How do I correctly love myself?" There's only one way. It's to believe that the Creator of the universe, the One Who flung the stars into space, the One Who put the planets into orbit, the One Who formed you in your mother's womb, this Creator, God Himself, has an affection for you. You're a glow-worm to Him. He gave you His Son.

In loving ourselves correctly, there's a big difference between loving ourselves and demanding that others love us. If we don't know

The Face of Grace

the love God has for our soul, for each of us; if we don't see how special we are, special enough that God would give us Himself that we might live, then what's going to happen is we're going to look for other people to love us.

It's like the old country and western song you've probably heard, we'll be "Looking for Love in all the Wrong Places." You'll be looking, I'll be looking for love in all the wrong places. If we're looking for love, demanding it from other people, we will have forgotten that we have all the love we need in the One Whose love counts. When we begin to understand and connect with God's love for us in the Lord Jesus Christ, we will begin to realize that He has a special affection for us that's found in no one else. It's as though He has our picture posted on His refrigerator. He loves us and He's concerned for us.

Loving ourselves means that we're free from the pressure of getting others to love us.

When we understand who we are by the grace of God, that the God of all grace has set His affection upon us and truly loves us, that He gave His Son for us and nothing will separate us from His love, we won't need anybody else's love.

Every one of us has experienced the rejection of somebody important to us. Somewhere along the line, someone looked at us and said, "I don't like you anymore. You're no good. I'm leaving. I'm done." I understand the hurt that comes from that. But let me emphasize, you don't need another human being's love when you understand how special you are in terms of God's love. The problem is that we talk about God's love all the time, but we really don't come to a settled peace that He truly thinks we're special. To love yourself is to know that God sees true worth in you.

You see, in the workplace your worth is based upon performance. Your wages are given to you based upon what your business says you're worth, and believe me, performance will wear you down. It will. But I understand why it's done that way. Capitalism is what drives performance in the workplace, and as I covered in the previous chapter, grace does not figure in the workplace.

By the way, in family situations it becomes a very difficult thing when a mom or dad obtain their worth and their esteem from the performance of their kids. It's very difficult to grow up in a home where parents are super-dependent on their kids. We live in a world where worth or value is predicated on performance, awards, college entrance exams and degrees and so on. It's so crazy, some parents might go to the extent of bribing a tennis coach to let their son or daughter onto the team, even though their child doesn't play tennis.

God says of us that He formed us in our mother's womb. He gave us breath. We each are a glow-worm to Him. He loves us so much He gave us His Son.

"We love Him because He first loved us" (I John 4:19). I propose to you that you cannot love God until you understand He loves you. If you ever feel a lack of energy to serve God, it may be because you're not captivated by the fact of His awesome, deep, unfathomable love for you.

If you go to a church where the motivation for doing what you do for God is based on shame, they will have lost the message of grace. If you understand who God is, the God of all grace, and what He's done for you, wild horses couldn't hold you back from bringing a foster child into your home, or from giving money to someone in need, or from encouraging young people going on a mission trip. Wild horses couldn't keep you from doing things like this. Why? Because you would have been captivated by the love of God. But here's the thing: you'll never love Him until you are consumed by His love for you.

To see the best in others is to see the worth of their personhood. We will never see the best in other people until we see their worth, and we can't see their worth until we know how much we are worth in the eyes of God. "Love your neighbor" (Matt. 22:39). Jesus said the second commandment is to love your neighbor, again, as yourself.

When you love yourself deeply, you can love others radically. Have you ever considered that? Did you grow up with messages in your mind like…Hey, you're no good. You can't ever do that. Who do you think you are? What's going on in your life? Perhaps you grew up with these tapes playing in your mind. You heard them from people that told you that you would never measure up. You frequently found yourself being "put in your place". You were never good enough. You were being compared to your brother or to your sister and so on. Then all of a sudden, the gospel of grace penetrates your heart. And God, the One who created you in your mother's womb says you are a glow-worm.

"God, You think so much of me You would die for me?" Yes. And that will never change. The Bible says love believes all things, love bears all things, love hopes all things, love endures all things. (I Corinthians 13:7) I propose to you that we're not going to bear burdens for a worm. We're not going to believe the words of a worm. We're not going to hope all things for a worm. But if somebody is a glow-worm, somebody really special, we are going to do whatever we can for that person. The next challenge is to focus on a person that's rejecting you. That hurtful person is one who's also been created in God's image.

When God created each of us, we were created in His image, so we were created as image bearers. Most of us had that image marred growing up. But redemption, salvation, is nothing but the God of all grace turning us back around into one who bears that full image of who He is. The image of God is not so much something that a person *bears* as it is something that a person *is*.

What that means is this: you've got somebody in your life who is rejecting you and it hurts, or somebody who thinks you're no good, or somebody who doesn't like you. How do you respond? Exactly the same way God responded to you when the whole world was telling you that you had no worth. The Creator loved you enough to die for you. For God so loved…(put your name here)…that He gave his only begotten Son for you. Wow!

Realize that lostness is a disconnect from the God of all grace. The "lostness" here is not somebody going to hell or judgment. I'm talking about somebody that's lost in life, somebody that got disconnected from their sense of personal worth in God. They've looked to you instead to try to get what they need. When that happens, just realize that person has worth too, but they've lost a sense of their own worth. That's why they're rejecting you.

You see, to be strong in life means that we stop believing the messages people tell us, and we start clinging to the truth of what God says. God says you're a glow-worm, a thing of wonder, beauty and delight. Do you believe that? You can be that person who connects a lost person to the grace of God. That person who is lost needs someone to bear the image of God to them, as in the old song, You're the Only Jesus Some Will Ever See.

Have you ever considered that God has called you into ministry? It may not be Executive Pastor at Emmanuel, it may not be the Lead Pastor at Emmanuel, but you've been called to the ministry. You know which ministry that is? That ministry is to show people how valuable they are. Even when they're unworthy, even when they're running, even when they're mean and nasty. Your ministry is to show that they have value.

Let's never allow our Christian lives to be lived in such a way that those who might be our enemies, or those that reject us, would say we don't show the spirit of grace. Our challenge is to realize that grace treats people in the same manner the God of all grace treats us. The eyes of grace see the best in everyone.

May we recognize the face of grace when we see it. And in those occasions of our lives when grace is not present, may God's words to us be just a checklist, a realization that we've simply lost a connection and understanding of who we are to Him. We've momentarily forgotten that loving people is the result of loving ourselves, and to love God is to be captivated by His love for us. May we see, comprehend and embrace the value and the worth of our personhood.

Chapter Eleven Discussion Questions

1. Do you recall childhood "tapes" of comments made to you, that might still be playing in your mind?
2. What would God be saying if it were Him making those comments instead?
3. We are created for relationship, with God and with others. How will a right understanding of our true worth help us in our relationships with others?
4. What actions show that we do in fact, see the best in others?

Chapter Twelve

"Eyes That Cover The Sins Of People"

1 Peter 4:8

"Love covers a multitude of sins."

I recently read a book by Jonathon Lehmann where he proposed that followers of Jesus like you and me follow the Lord Jesus, and we function like an embassy. The way he put it was that an embassy is a delegation of people who represent their home country while living in a foreign country, which is what believers in Christ are actually doing presently. Excellent point!

Now, if Jonathan Lehmann is correct and you and I serve as heaven's embassy, we then represent God the King of Kings, and our home country which is heaven, to the world in which we live. You and I are called as ambassadors to publicize our King's mindset and to proclaim our King's message. In other words, when people look at us, they should see God. When people hang around us, they should get a taste of heaven.

Have you ever considered that this is your calling in life? You may have asked yourself, what is my purpose? What should I do for a living? Where should I go to college? Who should I marry? Those are all important questions, but your major calling is to be an ambassador of Jesus Christ and represent Him in this world.

In First Peter 1:1, the apostle Peter writes to followers of Jesus like you and like me, "Peter, to those who reside as aliens…" And he says to those who reside as aliens, "Peace." Peter is writing to us, wishing us peace. But do you notice that he calls us aliens?

The Face of Grace

We're living in a day when our nation is constructing a wall in South Texas to keep out people from Mexico. It's a political hot potato, and I realize that some of you may be on one side of the proverbial fence and others on the other side as to whether or not we should keep aliens out. But have you ever considered that you yourself are an alien? That's right. You're living in America, but this is not your home country. You might say, "What do you mean?"

Peter writes in 1:4, "to those with an inheritance in heaven." The place where you receive your inheritance, that is your home. Earthly inheritances sometimes have a way of driving families apart. Brothers and sisters can become enemies over disagreements about how an inheritance should be passed down. Let's stop thinking about our earthly inheritance because earth isn't our home. Our home is heaven and we've been given our inheritance there. Jesus is building for us a home right now, a home in which we will live for eternity. He has made us by our faith in Him, a co-heir with Him, and it is there that we are given all the blessings that Jesus earned in His life.

When we set our eyes on heaven where our home really is, and we understand that we're aliens in this world, then we'll begin to understand what it means to be an ambassador of the King of all Kings.

Peter goes on in 2:11, "I urge you as sojourners and exiles." A sojourner is a person who is on a journey. You and I are on a journey. We're on our way to our ultimate home. But right now, we're aliens. We are exiles and sojourners. We know Jesus, but we're living in a foreign land among people who don't know Him or claim Him as King.

Peter writes his letter to you and to me and he says, "Do whatever the King desires. Live your life as an alien, an exile, a sojourner. Live your life according to the King's wishes." You may say, "Well, what does the King want from me?" The answer is in I Peter. Oh, my!

It's amazing. We discover there what God desires of us as we serve as His ambassadors in a foreign country. Peter closes his wonderful book with a verse in Chapter 4, which is the text for this study as Peter outlines the King's wishes for us. I Peter 4:8, "Above all, keep fervent in your love for one another, because love covers a multitude of sins."

In this *Face of Grace* study, we have seen that you know me because you recognize my face. I know you because I recognize your face. As followers of Jesus we talk about grace, we sing about it. But my question again is, what does grace look like? What is the face of grace? Can we recognize it, and will others recognize it?

If the Bible says that God is the God of all grace (and it does), and if the Scripture says He's called us into His kingdom (and He has), then we are ambassadors for Him in this foreign land. As God's ambassadors, you and I are to have His eyes,

---

Eyes with the kind of loving grace, That Cover the Sins of People

---

This doesn't mean that we cover up crimes against children or we protect predators when they cross those appropriate and legal boundaries and abuse another person. Oh, no, we stop that in its tracks! No! We prevent that. When we say grace covers a multitude of sins, it means we cover those sins committed against us. What this means is that as a follower of Jesus Christ and as an ambassador of the King, one who represents His message in a foreign land, I will show you by my life that I will cover your sins against me because "love keeps no record of wrongs" (I Corinthians 13:5 NIV).

I want you to think about what happened to you this week, maybe last month, maybe even a year ago. Some of you perhaps couldn't even sleep last night because you were hurt by something that had happened to you. It could be that someone who committed to love you "until death do you part" has abandoned you. It could be that you were unjustly fired from your job. It may be that somebody lied about you, slandered you, gossiped about you to other people, and you are hurt because you have discovered this.

Does this describe you? The King of all grace is saying to you, "Keep no record of the wrong done against you." You may be thinking, "Oh, that's easy for you to say." I do understand how you feel. I've looked at my own life and thought to myself, "What would prevent me from genuinely not keeping any record of wrong that someone else has committed against me?"

What might stop me from keeping a list of the things that others have done that caused me hurt at some time in my life? What would prevent me from doing what the King says, from being a person of grace to others? What would obstruct me from living out the message of grace, the message of my God in a foreign land?

I came up with four things.

First, I must know that the God of all grace keeps no record of my wrongs. It's as simple as this: If I think He keeps a record of my wrongs, then it's guaranteed I'm going to keep a record of your wrongs. But if my King, the King of all grace says to me, "Wade, I keep no list of your wrongs," then because I'm His ambassador, I can show you that I have no list of your wrongs.

You may be thinking, "I don't know that I believe that. I don't know that I believe God keeps no record of my sins."

Eyes That Cover the Sins of People

Well, how about this? Romans 3:24, "We are justified freely by his grace through the redemption that is in Jesus Christ." Do you see the word *justified* there? Do you know what that means? It's a big fancy theological word, but its meaning is really simple. Justified means to be treated *just as if I* never sinned.

God treats me just as if I never sinned because through his Son, the Lord Jesus Christ, He gave me redemption. He took my sins and put them upon the Lord Jesus, and Jesus paid for them in His death, burial, and resurrection, conquering both sin and death. So now, because my faith and trust are in Him, God justifies me. He treats me just as if I've never sinned. He justifies me. He has no record or list of my wrongs.

You may ask, "But don't we have to confess our sins? And doesn't sin hurt us? Yes, of course. But listen to what the word *confession* means. Confession is the Greek word *homolegeo*. *Legeo* means to speak. Homo means the same. Homosexual, the same sex. Homonym, the same sound. Homogenous, the same origin. When you confess your sin, you *homolegeo* it to God. You say the same thing about it that God says.

Here's an example of saying the same thing that God says, "Father, when I lied to my wife, that was wrong. But Father, thank you that You took my sin upon my Savior, and that you conquered it for me and that you treat me as if I have never sinned. Lord, thank you for my justification in the redemption that is found in Jesus Christ. Thank you that you keep no record of my wrongs. Now, Father, help me to make right what I've done that has hurt my wife."

That's confession.

If you go through life thinking that you've got to make up to God for what you've done wrong, you're going to find yourself going through life keeping a list of the wrongs done against you by other

The Face of Grace

people, and they're going to have to right these wrongs for you. But, if you come to the settled peace that the God of all grace has taken care of all of your sins, then you can be His ambassador in a foreign land doing the same for the people in your life.

You may ask, "I understand that He forgave me my sins when I came to Him the first time in faith, but what about all the sins I've committed since then?"

My answer to your question is simply this, how many of our sins were "future sins" when Jesus died for them on the cross? And the answer is: all of them. So, though we may make a distinction between past, present, and future, the God of all grace has taken care of the list of our sins at Calvary. Now He calls us to be an ambassador of His grace to other people.

Going back to my questions: What would prevent me from doing what the King says, from being a person of grace to others? What would obstruct me from living out the message of grace, the message of my God in a foreign land, knowing that the God of all grace keeps no record of my wrongs against him?

The second thing is, I must know that the God of all grace never wastes my experiences or my sorrows.

The reason you and I keep lists of wrongs done against us is because we're really upset with the people who've hurt us, so we keep a list because we either need payback or we've got to make sure that it never happens again because it hurt so badly. Also, we have forgotten what the Bible teaches us, that the King of Kings will make sure that everything in our life, good or bad, ultimately works for our good (Romans 8:28).

When Joseph was sold into slavery by his brothers, can you imagine how that must have hurt? This was his own flesh and blood! They were going to kill him, then they sold him to the Egyptians as a

Eyes That Cover the Sins of People

slave. Decades later after he spends time in prison while in Egypt, falsely accused of rape, he gets out of prison. He's eventually exalted to second in command of the large empire of Egypt.

In this prominent role he's in charge of food distribution, and next thing you know, his own brothers come down because they need food. They don't even know he's alive. They don't recognize him. He's got a beard, speaks a different language, he's got longer hair and a tan. When they ask this powerful Egyptian, or at least they think he's an Egyptian, for food, their brother reveals himself to them and says, "I am your brother, Joseph." The Bible then records, and it's interesting in the Hebrew, that the brothers of Joseph became so scared that their knees literally buckled. They shook, they wavered, they fell before this powerful man and they pled for mercy. His brothers expected that all this time, Joseph must have kept a list of the wrongs they had done against him all those years before.

Joseph commanded, "Get up. Get off your knees. Get up. Don't be scared. Don't be afraid of me. As for you, you meant evil. But God intended it for good. Do not be afraid" (Genesis 50:20).

The experience of Joseph is a good lesson for us. You see, we don't have to keep lists when we understand that even the hurt that comes our way is nothing but the God of all grace working ultimate good for us, even if we make mistakes, even if we go to prison for those mistakes. The good news is our God who loves us, the God of all grace, will work it out for our good even if we're falsely accused.

"And we know that God causes all things to work together for good" (Romans 8:28). Hmmmm… Do you not know? Do we not know that God causes all things to work together for our good? That's how I can refrain from keeping a list of wrongs that others have committed against me. I know God's working those wrongs for good.

Third, I must know that the God of all grace turns me from being self-absorbed into being selfless. When we become an ambassador of the King of all grace, we cease being a self-absorbed person and we become a selfless person.

The Scripture says, "Rescue the weak and the needy; deliver them from the hand of the wicked" (Psalm 82:4). We go for the protection of the innocent. We come to the defense of children. We do whatever it takes. We give whatever it takes in order for us to make sure we are defending the needy and the helpless.

But when it comes to you and me, we are neither needy nor are we helpless. Why? Because we each are an ambassador of the King of Kings, and He's on our side. He will turn all things for our good, so, we are not powerless victims. What we will do is we will see that God is at work in life, and we will be looking out for other people because we know the King has our back. We stop being self-absorbed and we start becoming selfless.

Fourth, I must know that the God of all grace is as much interested in what I *don't* do as what I do. Here's what I mean by that. In I Corinthians 13:5, "love keeps no record of wrongs" is the way Paul writes it.

Wow.

Do you know what a list-keeper is? A list-keeper is a person who keeps a record. If we're an ambassador of the King of all grace, then we live in this alien country as a sojourner and one in exile. We are to refuse to keep a list of wrong doings done against us. Why? Because that's exactly what God does for us.

List-keepers though, tend to keep records and they use absolute language when it comes to their relationships with other people. Here's the kind of language that is used. "I would never do that…What you just did to me, I would never do that to you…Why

Eyes That Cover the Sins of People

do you always…? I will always…!" Do you hear the absolute words *never* and *always*?

You see, because they have a list, list-keepers are thinking of that list so that when somebody does something wrong, it becomes "You never do what's right." I can prove that with my list, so the language is, "You always do what's wrong?" How do I know? Because I've got a list that I've been keeping and you're on it. Personally, I do my best to keep a very short list, because God is really interested in whether or not Wade Burleson keeps a list of other people's wrongs.

A person's lists prove that list-keepers relate based on performance. On the one hand, a list keeper will tell you, "Man, I'd love to go to lunch with you if you would just do what's right." "Man, I'll come to Christmas holiday. I'll be there, if you will treat me the way you should be treating me."

On the other hand, those who don't keep a record of wrongs are going to invite to lunch the person who slandered them. They're going to go visit that relative who's cranky and bitter and mean. Why? Because they have no list of that relative having been cranky, bitter, or mean the year before.

List-keepers can't trust, either. They've got to protect. By the way, the world is full of list-keepers. This is why it's an alien country to us. This is why we're sojourners. This is why we're in exile. The list-keepers of this world protect themselves, so they are very slow to trust others.

It's the old saying. "Fool me once, shame on you. Fool me twice, shame on me." That's a list-keeper's motto because they've got you. "Fool me once and I'll write it down. You fool me twice, my bad because I'd already written it down. But know this, I will never let you fool me again." Can you recall what Jesus said to his disciples? They came to him asking, "How often do we forgive people?" They just wanted Jesus to tell them how often they needed to forgive a person who wronged them in the same manner.

How many times do we have to forgive the same sin? Jesus said, "I tell you, not seven times in a day. Seventy times seven" (Matthew 18:22). Seventy times seven in Hebrew literature is a phrase that speaks of infinity. In other words, there is no stopping to forgiving somebody who wrongs you, even if it's the same sin over and over and over again. You say, how can that happen? How can I forgive someone who constantly struggles with the same thing in wounding me, in speaking against me, in a sin that's committed against me? How can I forgive them over and over and over and over again?

That's a great question. Are you ready for the answer? If you have no list, it's always the first time. Isn't that amazing? The reason we struggle with grace is because we think people should be different, and we act like we are their judge. But when we keep no list or record of wrongs, we actually become like the loving, forgiving God of grace to them.

List-keepers hurt because they are hurt. I recently had a good meeting with a couple that had been coming to Refuge. And the gentleman, much like me, like you, has made some poor choices in life. He shared with me some of those poor choices. Then he got a little teary and he said, "Pastor Wade, my wife said to me, 'I don't care what you've done. I want to show you grace.' " So, this gentleman, with tears coming down his cheeks said to me, "You know, I want to change. But it's not to obtain love. I want to change because I'm beginning to understand what it means to be loved."

When you cease being a list-keeper, when you can see people in your life that have wronged you without keeping record of it, when you are simply serving as an ambassador of the King to them, I propose to you the power of that life will transform people around you.

There's nothing like being in the presence of a true ambassador of the God of all grace.

May this message of grace and what it looks like, resonate in each of our hearts.

Chapter Twelve Discussion Questions

1. How easy is it to forgive a person "seventy times seven"?
2. Are there certain offenses that are harder for you to forgive than others? How does God view the more difficult offenses?
3. Why do persons of grace not need to keep a list of wrongs committed against us?
4. What sort of freedom comes to the list-keeper that no longer keeps a list? What about for the persons that were on that list?

Chapter Thirteen

"Eyes That Avoid The Craving For People"

Philippians 4:19
"My God will supply all your needs…"

I grew up in a fundamental Baptist church. My father, whom I consider to be my best friend, was the pastor of that church when I was young, and he was pretty legalistic, although he's not that way now. Church was all about performance, and I grew up with an understanding of God that was not healthy. I understood God as being someone who demanded performance from me before He would even think about blessing me. This experience left me scarred.

In fact, I can remember that this church had a long list of do's and don'ts, and the don't list was definitely longer. You don't dance. You definitely don't smoke. You don't drink at all. You don't go to movies if they're rated PG or worse. The list contained rules like that. The older I got, the more I realized something wasn't right, and in time I began to question. Now before you ask, my dad didn't stay this way forever. He underwent a remarkable transformation later in life, which I will talk about in a later chapter.

I discovered something very ironic after I grew up and left this fundamental Baptist church. The first time Baptists sent missionaries overseas, they planned it out in an ale house. It was a place they owned, and they even brewed their own ale because they couldn't find work anywhere else in England. They were today's quintessential nonconformists. I thought, how does that jive with what I know now, or at least what I've been taught constitutes true Christianity?

The Face of Grace

I discovered as I became a pastor that a lot of times, churches and pastors develop their lists of sins based upon the prevailing culture, and it has nothing to do with the Scriptures. For example, in Oklahoma some people say studies have suggested that our Native American friends have difficulty physically processing the chemical of alcohol. Whether this is true or not, what those researchers have found is that alcohol is broken down and eliminated differently in Native Americans than in other populations. I think Prohibition was partially the outgrowth of that kind of thinking. Regardless, labeling drinking a sin was a solution that Baptists helped come up with to solve this problem. The only thing is, when we make those lists of sins as if they come from God, and then say God is going to punish you if any of these sins are present in your life, we end up with a warped view of God.

I don't often talk about sin or bring messages about our sins, your sins and my sins. I'm not sure I ever have, but if I have, it hasn't been often. In our study now, though, I'm going to talk about our sins.

It might surprise you that I don't have a list. I really don't. In fact, there's really only one sin in my life that I fight every day, and it's the exact same sin in your life that you fight. It's the sin of idolatry. That's it! You are probably thinking, "What? Are you kidding me? Idolatry?" You see, when we think of idolatry today or we read about it in Scripture, we think of little statues, gods if you will, of stone and of wood that ancient people used to worship. Since we think like that, we think we don't have any struggle with idolatry because we are sure we serve the true God.

Here's one example. In Genesis 31:34 we read, "Now Rachel had taken her father's household idols and hidden them in her saddle, and she was sitting on them. And Laban searched for them." We come across a passage like this one, and that's how we think of idolatry. We remember the first commandment of the old covenant,

Eyes That Avoid the Craving for People

"Thou shalt have no other gods before me" (Exodus 20:3). That's what God commanded. So, we tell ourselves that we don't struggle with idolatry because we don't have an ancient idol like they did in Biblical times. That's so unfortunate, because even the ancients didn't think of idolatry the way we are thinking of it. Let me explain.

I study history, so I understand how the ancient Mesopotamians, Assyrians, Greeks and Romans worshipped their gods, and they had many gods. The Greeks had Artemis, the goddess of fertility and the hunt. The Greeks also had Zeus, the god of lightning and thunder. The Romans had Jupiter. They had Mars, the god of the message. He was the messenger. These were the big gods.

The ancients would make little statues that were physical representations of the invisible and distant gods that they couldn't see literally. But none of them thought of the idol as their god. No, no, no. They thought of it like a picture, something that reminded them of their invisible and distant God. The ancients would pray to their gods the same way that Laban would pray to his Mesopotamian gods. He would speak to the invisible god, but it would be to the idol that represented that god. The ancients considered those stone and wood statues to be very powerful.

We see some of that tradition in modern days. For instance, in the country of Haiti they have what we call voodoo dolls, and their function is very similar to the statue idols of the ancient peoples. It's a doll that represents another person. What the Haitians will do even today if they're involved in voodoo is to take that doll, knowing that it's not the person but an image representing the person who is distant, and they'll poke a pin in it to cause that person pain. That's the idea the ancients had about their idols.

Again, you may say in response, "Well, I don't struggle with idolatry because I don't own any gods of stone or wood." And I would respond, "Well, yes, you do, and so do I." It's our great sin. But rather than having idols of wood and stone, our idols are usually people, flesh and blood. These are people who bleed. People who cry. People we love. And when the God of all grace calls us into His family, He begins to remove idolatry from our life.

In this *Face of Grace* study, we're learning that God is the God of all grace. He loves us even when we are unworthy. He pursues us when we are not seeking Him. He embraces us when we're not perfect. He finishes what He begins in us, which is the work of grace, even when we fail to fulfill our commitment to Him. When we begin to understand who God really is, we realize we've never met anybody like Him.

The problem is that we grow up in churches, and still we really never know God. Because of that, we start looking for other gods, and that usually involves people. I want us to see that God in His love for us, as He continues His work of grace in us, will give us:

Eyes that, Avoid the Craving for People

Do you realize that for most of us, when we haven't yet come to an understanding of who God is to us and how wonderful He truly is, we depend on people for our identity? For ladies, maybe it's your husband. You carry his name. Your entire identity is associated mostly with him and his family. Mom, maybe it's your daughters or your sons. It's the idea that you're the mom of some wonderful kids. That's your identity. Dad, maybe it's that boss that you are a friend with, or that guy who has a lot of influence that you like to spend time around.

Eyes That Avoid the Craving for People

When we don't know who God really is, we struggle with idolatry, specifically, the idolatry of other people. Leslie Vernick, author of The Emotionally Destructive Relationship: Seeing it, Stopping it, Surviving it, says, "When you give another person the power to define you, then you also give them the power to control you." The only person who should be controlling your life is the God of all grace. But if we don't know who God is, we will look to people and depend on them for that purpose.

Moms, this may particularly hit you hard. You have these kids you're raising, and they provide your purpose in life. You invest yourself in them. And by the way, rarely do I ever meet a bad mom. I know they're out there, and some of you may have had a bad mom, but frankly, that's a rarity in my experience. There is something about a mother's love that is mystical and transcendent; it is something that is amazing. But what happens is this: when the kids get older and leave the nest, a mom's life radically changes. Purpose is gone.

Husbands, say you lose your job, you're no longer employed. People think of you as an unemployed man. It really bothers you, right? Why is that? I propose to you that we get our sense of purpose from our work and from people, and that's not the way God would have it. He wants us to define our life by our relationship with Him. That's who we are.

Our co-dependency is basically an inappropriate over-the-top loyalty, caring and supportiveness to people. We often don't see it in our lives because we say things like, oh, I just really love that person. Yes, but it's over the top because you're not truly loving that person, you're in fact loving yourself. You want your daughter to be who *you* want her to be, not for her sake but for yours. You want your son to be the star athlete, not for his sake but to meet your own needs or wishes. You want your husband to reflect what you want him to be in the community, maybe not as much for his sake as for your own. Husbands, maybe you feel the same toward your wives. That's codependency. It's idolatry. And God is doing a work in all of us, working to separate us from our sin.

Matthew 1:21, "...you shall call His name Jesus." For this is the reason you call him Jesus. "He shall save His people from their sins." What? He will save us from our sins. This includes the sin of idolatry. Idolatry. That's it.

> We fall into idolatry when we don't know who God is and we depend on people for our security, our sense of stability.

The God of all grace wants you to know who He is, and then to depend upon Him. Depend on His love for you and what He does as He begins His work of grace in you. What that means is you become a Christian, a follower of Jesus. God is the one who initiated that. I realize that you think you initiated it. The old evangelist Dwight L. Moody was famous for saying, "On top of the door where you enter into the Kingdom of Christ is the phrase 'Whosoever will, let him come.' But then when you walk through the door of the Kingdom and turn around, you see the words of Jesus, 'You have not chosen me, but I have chosen you.'" The work that He has begun in us is one of teaching us to be sufficient and secure in Him, finding our identity and our purpose in Him.

In Philippians 4:19 Paul writes, "And my God will supply all your needs according to His riches in glory in Christ Jesus."

"My God", Paul says. Who is this God? He's not the God that's about to beat you down. He's not the God that is measuring you based upon your performance. He is not the God that you may have grown up with in religion. No, no, no. He's the God of all grace. That's the God Paul says is his God. He's my God. He's your God.

Let me remind you: Anybody who has ever had a job for pay where you signed an employment contract performed for pay and received a performance review at least annually, if not quarterly. Your performance was measured in terms of how well you carried out your responsibilities. Maybe you got a bonus, but if you didn't perform well, you might have been fired. We've all experienced that kind of performance evaluation.

The sad thing is we carry that concept over into our relationship with God. We think that when we became a Christian, we signed a contract of employment. So, we perform for God expecting He'll bless us if we perform well, and if we don't, well, frankly we're a little scared of Him so we hide from Him. You get a guy that's struggling with things in his private life. He'll never go to church because why would he want to go to church to hear about a God that's really going to "get him" this week? He'd just as soon ignore that God and turn to his idols.

This verse says that my God, that your God who is all grace, will supply our every need according to his riches in glory. Notice it doesn't say according to our performance. My God of all grace shall supply my every need according to His riches. We have to be careful not to carry the concept of a performance contract over to our relationship with God. This verse simply means the following: God providentially knows what we need, and He vows to meet our every need!

That is stunning. I can't do that. I can't make that promise. You can't make that promise to anybody else. Only the Creator of the universe, Who flung the stars and sustains every atom, only He can promise to know our every need and meet it. And He does.

If we really understood who He is and what He's promised us, we would never be anxious for anything. Not for anything! Philippians 4:6 says, "Do not be anxious about anything, but in everything by prayer and supplication with thanksgiving let your requests be made known to God."

In fact, if you will make every request you have based upon what your concept of your needs are, you make them known to the Lord through communion. That is prayer, talking to God, and through your supplication, that's a big fancy word that simply means you will "supply" to God what's on your heart, you'd just let Him know. Like a friend would to a trusted friend. And He will meet your needs.

Notice Philippians 4:6 says we are to make our request known with thanksgiving. Why with thanksgiving? Because we already know the promise that He is going to meet our every need. In fact, John Piper in his book Desiring God says, "If we live by faith in God's promise of future grace, it will be very hard for anxiety to survive." You see, the reason I get anxious and the reason you get anxious is because we have lost sight that God is the God of all grace. He promises to meet our every need according to His riches, not according to our performance. Too often we step back into the mentality that God will meet our needs based upon our performance. If we're not performing well, bad things happen, and if we are performing well, good things will happen.

There's a problem with this mentality. If good things don't happen when we're performing well, we often get really, really angry with God and think, "I've done everything I said I would do." And your loving Heavenly Father basically responds to you with something that might sound like this, "Listen, I've got your back. Every need you have, I will meet. That's a promise I'm making to you according to My riches, not your worthiness. But what I'm going to do is I'm going to show you that every other idol in your life is a false idol that leads you to harm and ultimate ruin. Trust me."

God's promise is to supply all your needs according to His riches in glory. Again, not your performance. The word *supply* in the Greek means "to cram completely full." It means He doesn't just meet the need, whatever need you have, He goes beyond it. He does exceedingly abundantly more than you could ever imagine or think. That's a promise, by the way. (Ephesians 3:20)

Some of you might be thinking right now, "Okay. I need a Ferrari. I need a bigger house." No, you don't! What you need is somebody who loves you unconditionally. You need Him. All those other things are idols. And by the way, one of the things that I've observed is that when people who know and follow Jesus become wealthy, their money never becomes their god. There's no idolatry, and oftentimes they get more. But for the wealthy who don't know God, the money becomes their god and they want more, but it usually ends in their ruin. There is a way that seems right to man, the Scripture says, but the end thereof is the way of death. (Proverbs 14:12)

Here's the thing for those of you who have embraced Jesus. You have a God of all grace Who has promised to meet your every need. Colossians 1:27 says, "To whom God willed to make known the riches of the glory of this mystery among the Gentiles; which is Christ in you, the hope of glory." "To whom," this means you and me. God willed to make known the riches of the glory of this mystery among the Gentiles, which is Christ in you, the hope of glory. All that verse means is that God intends to show us His goodness in Jesus and teach us by His grace. We need nothing but Him.

You're perhaps thinking to yourself, "Listen, I've embraced Jesus but I'm not sure how much I know about Him. I'm not sure how much faith I have or how strong it is." Don't let that stress you out. It's not the amount or quality of your faith that counts. What matters is where your faith is placed. And if it is in the God of all grace who gave you His Son, that's enough, no matter how small or weak your faith is. It might be the case that your faith is in Jesus, but you're

The Face of Grace

thinking to yourself, "Wait, wait, wait. Some really tough, bad things have happened in my life."

Yes, bad things happen to good folks. I have friends whose son was murdered by his wife's boyfriend. Their son's wife then took the kids and fled to Mexico, but she was eventually caught. When I performed their son's funeral, the hurt and the brokenness in their hearts was hard to bear.

Recently I was with a family who was by the bedside of their critically ill mother that had just had heart surgery and wasn't doing well. I was praying with the husband, and afterward he tearfully said, "Wade, I wouldn't want to wish anything like this on anyone else." Such pain. So hard to understand.

I understand some of you may be going through some pain right now. Maybe it's the abandonment of someone who pledged to love you. Maybe it's the rejection of a son who has not talked to you for a long time. Maybe it's family members, siblings who have turned against you, who want nothing to do with you. Maybe it's your reputation. People have said things about you, forget whether it's true or false, it's just everybody saying things about you, and your reputation is sullied. I wouldn't want to wish any of that on anyone.

All of this is hurtful to bear, but, contrary to your thoughts it isn't punishment. No. The God of all grace is at work in your life removing idols you've put there.

We were driving down I-35 a few years ago at 70 miles an hour. I was in a Honda Accord, the car that I like to drive, with Rachelle in the passenger seat. We were going the speed limit but an overloaded truck, its tail lights pointed down, was in the right-hand lane going 15 miles an hour. We slammed into the rear of the truck and the guardrail, demolishing my car and injuring my wife. She had to undergo

Eyes That Avoid the Craving for People

surgery in the hospital in Oklahoma City. My wife, a seamstress and sewing store owner in downtown Enid came away with severely injured fingers that are still crooked to this day. Her knee was swollen, requiring surgery as well.

I was standing out there in the middle of the highway with a totaled car, my wife injured, waiting for first responders to come and get her out. People from Enid were driving by because we'd all just attended a high school basketball game where our son was playing. I wouldn't want to wish that on anyone. But I know my God, and this was not a punishment from Him.

God's presence in your time of need will bring you comfort until your need is met. He promises us in Isaiah 41:10, "Fear not (the Lord says), for I am with you. Be not dismayed. I will strengthen you. I will help you."

You know, looking back on our accident, and looking back on whatever has happened in your life, we might wonder sometimes, God, why? Why? Here's the answer. The Lord in His love for you is not wasting any circumstance. He's not throwing away any tear you have shed. He is coming into your house, in love for you, and removing your idols like Rachel removed her father's idols in Genesis 31.

We think life is all about comfort and security, protection, and all the nice things that everybody enjoys. Turn on MTV, watch television. It's all about who's the most popular, who looks the best, who dresses the finest, who has the most. That will all end in destruction because it's false idol worship. What God is doing in His love for us is saying "I'm removing it all from you so that you can know that I alone am enough."

Some of you might say, "But I don't want Him to remove it from me." That's my point. Each of us needs to come to the place of saying, "Lord, whatever comes my way, You are enough because I know you've promised to meet my needs according to Your riches. And if I don't have it, I don't need it." Many of us were not raised or taught that, but I really believe if you search it out for yourself in Scripture, you will see I am not misleading you.

As the God of all grace walks with you through your days, may you learn to hear Him saying, "I've got your back. I know what you need. Trust Me. If you don't know why you're going through what you're going through, whatever it is, just trust Me until you see it is because I know what you really need." May this truth live in the hearts of each of us!

Chapter Thirteen Discussion Questions

1. What modern-day idols are available to satisfy our "craving" for people?
2. How is God's "contract" with us different from a "contract" with an employer?
3. Why should we make our requests known to God with an attitude of thanksgiving, instead of an attitude of anxiety?
4. What will give the graced person comfort in the event they face a detour in life, or prayers that don't get answered the way they hoped or wanted?

Chapter Fourteen

"Eyes That Focus on the Needs of People"

Galatians 6:1-2
"Bear one another's burdens, and so fulfill the law of Christ."

Over the course of the last few chapters, we've been exploring what grace looks like. We know how to recognize one another, and we're learning to recognize God's grace beyond just singing about it in church. But how does grace look in our lives? The Bible says that the God of all grace has called us into His kingdom. We are to reflect Him. God is conforming us into His image, which means we should be persons of all grace. But what does that look like?

I want to show you that a graced person has

Eyes that,

Focus on the Needs of People

Let's look at the book of Galatians, Chapter 6. Martin Luther, the great reformer who lived in the 16th century, called Galatians "my Katie von Bora." Luther was married to Katie. He called Galatians "my Katie von Bora" because he was wed to this book of Scripture. He loved it. All of Luther's life, he was resisting religious leaders who were telling followers of Jesus to tithe this, to do that, to commit to this and that. Luther resisted them and said, no, no, no. We need to first be captured by the grace of God and then live graciously. Galatians tells us how to live graced lives.

The Face of Grace

The Apostle Paul wrote the book of Galatians and, like every book, he writes the first few chapters in terms of a doctrine, showing who God is and what He's done for us. Halfway through Galatians, Paul makes a switch. Even the verbs change. In the latter half of Galatians, the verbs become imperative verbs, which means they are commands for followers of Jesus, commands to obey. So, is Paul saying a graced person is to do certain things? Yes.

This is one of them. Galatians 6:1-2, "1Brethren, even if anyone is caught in any trespass, you who are spiritual, restore such a one in a spirit of gentleness; each one looking to yourself, so that you too will not be tempted. 2 Bear one another's burdens, and thereby fulfill the law of Christ."

I'm going to show you from these two verses some things about our lives and what that means for us. How we should live. What grace looks like.

Working on behalf of those trapped by destructive behaviors is grace at work. Recently, an article was published in the local newspaper about the ministry that several of our lay people run, called Free World. We bring in men and women who are locked up in prison. We're certified to do that, and through this ministry they've become our friends. When they are released, many of them stay in Enid and we help them find jobs. They move their families up here.

Some of our members meet with several men who are now out of prison living in the Oasis Center that we helped build. They are just loving these men where they are, and we looked at hiring one or two of them as custodians here at Emmanuel. Any time we employ someone, we have a policy where we will run a background check. Sometimes the background checks that come back for these men are fairly full. It's called a rap sheet, and you'll see all kinds of problems these men have had with the law since they were teenagers.

Eyes That Focus on the Needs of People

Sadly, some Baptist churches would thumb their nose at these men and women and say they have no use for them. If you're ever in a church like that, you're not in a grace church. But when you find a group of people like Emmanuel, who recognize that helping men and women who've been caught in destructive behavior is what grace looks like, don't ever leave that church. They are doing what Christ has called the church to do.

Now, let me show you a few things about this work of helping people out of their destructive behaviors.

First, this is "physician" work, not detective work.

Many churches are populated by nosy detectives, when what we need are loving physicians. When Galatians 6:1 says, "Therefore, brethren, you who are spiritual, if you come across anyone caught in a trespass," the word *caught* there doesn't mean, aha, I caught you, you can't hide that from me… That's not what that word means at all.

The word *caught* is the same word used by the writer of Hebrews where he says in Chapter 12: "[1]Therefore, since we have so great a cloud of witnesses surrounding us, let us also lay aside every encumbrance and the sin which so easily (here is that word) entangles us, and let us run with endurance the race that is set before us, [2]fixing our eyes on Jesus, the author and perfecter of faith, who for the joy set before Him endured the cross, despising the shame, and has sat down at the right hand of the throne of God."

My point is that sometimes you will know people who get caught or entangled in a trespass. You know what the word trespass means? Of course you do, if you are farmers or hunters that is. You've got a fence out there, right? And you'll put a sign on there that says No…what? No Trespassing. A trespass is an intentional act to cross an appropriate boundary.

Did you realize that the Bible says sometimes people are caught and entangled by intentionally crossing appropriate boundaries? Some of you might say to yourself, "Listen, if I ever knew anyone that saw a No Trespassing sign and crossed that fence, he would get what's coming to him." Is that your attitude? Well, you might need to change it, because the trespass here is an intentional act. People get entangled by their trespasses, and what you're to do is to restore the individual.

This is delicate work, not forceful work, meaning you're not a detective, you're a physician. So, let's say you see someone caught up and entangled in a trespass. Maybe they've left their spouse for a girlfriend or for a boyfriend. Maybe they were caught smoking marijuana at a stop sign and got arrested. Maybe it's someone who was arrested for a DUI and it's in the local newspaper. Maybe it's something that is not in the paper, but everybody in your card group is talking about it. It's a trespass, an intentional act. You and I are to be gentle, not punitive. Notice the word restore in Galatians 6:1. "We are to restore that person" comes from the medical field in ancient Greece. It was used by the Greeks to describe repairing a broken bone.

When I was a sophomore in high school, I played quarterback for Southwest High School, a big school in Fort Worth, Texas. We were playing for the district championship when I broke my left arm on the third play of the game. I stayed in the game, playing the entire game. Thankfully I'm right-handed, so I was throwing with my right while I'd suffered the injury in my left arm taking a snap.

I didn't tell anybody that I was hurt. My dad could tell though, as he watched from the stands.

It was only after the game that the coaches asked what the problem was. I said I had hurt my arm. So, we went to the doctor and they x-rayed it to discover it was fractured. The doctor couldn't believe that I had fractured my left arm in the third play of the

Eyes That Focus on the Needs of People

game. I wish I could describe for you how delicately this physician set my arm. He was extremely gentle as he carefully and tenderly restored my arm.

I felt like saying to him, "You know, Doc, I've played an entire game with a broken arm. Why are you so gentle?" But I understood why. When you're a physician who sees someone injured by what they've been caught up in, you're going to treat them gently. On the other hand, if you're a detective or a police officer, you may catch someone who requires punishment. Graced persons of God are physicians, not prosecutors. This is what Paul means when he says, "You who are spiritual, restore such a one in a spirit of gentleness" (Galatians 6:1).

One of the most valuable things I've learned about a broken bone is that a restored, mended bone is stronger than a bone that has never been fractured. If you ever find a church that helps people caught up in their trespasses, you'll end up finding people later on that are stronger in their own lives than if they'd never been caught up in their trespass in the first place. This work that we're called to do is a healing work, not a punitive work. We're called to heal.

It's a little bit like Jesus when he met the woman at the well. She'd been married five times. She was living with a man who was not her husband. Jesus spoke to her gently and tenderly. The conversation was quite remarkable. Jesus was doing something that the religious Jews of His day would never have dreamed of doing. He conveyed grace to this woman. That's the way we're to be when we encounter those that are caught in a trespass.

Let me show you a second thing. Working to help others escape destructive patterns requires a personal diligence. It's interesting that in Verse 1 there is a shift from the plural first person "you who are spiritual" in the beginning, to the singular first person (you) at the end.

"Each one looking to yourself, so that you too will not be tempted"(Galatians 6:1b).

In other words, the best work for restoring people who have been caught in trespasses is a corporate work of all of us. You can't have prisoners living in your house, but we corporately can build a place where prisoners when they get out, can live. You can't do everything for everybody, but corporately, as a body we might be able to do far more than you could ever dream. That's a corporate work.

Recently, a pastor from another church along with twelve members from their missions and community ministry came to Enid and visited with us about what we are doing in our community and in missions. As they left they said, "You tell your people we are shocked. We are amazed at what Emmanuel is doing." I told them I would. Corporately, it's the best work we could be doing. It is one of the reasons why the last five years of Emmanuel have been extraordinary for me, because I really feel like we've hit that sweet spot of what we should be doing.

Corporately, we are to restore those caught in a trespass in a spirit of gentleness. But personally, you and I are to watch out for ourselves, each of us individually. We're just like everybody else. In order for you and for me to be effective in restoring those caught up in trespasses, we have to be diligent about our own lives. In other words, I want to help other people, but I'm going to make sure that I'm not caught up in the trespass.

We see that working to help others caught up in sin is a fulfillment of the law of Christ. Pay careful attention to Verse 2 so there's no confusion, and also because some of you didn't grow up with this kind of mentality. Verse 2 reads: "Bear one another's burdens, and thereby fulfill the law of Christ" (6:2).

Eyes That Focus on the Needs of People

Now, what "burden" is being mentioned here? The burden here is not necessarily the burden of poverty. It might include that, and we will do our part. The burden here is not necessarily the burden of sickness, but we do our part to minister in that as well. In context, the burden that we are to bear in Verse 2 is the burden of a flagrant trespass, a sin that someone has been caught up in. When you bear that burden, you're fulfilling the law of Christ.

Let me show you what I mean. What is the law of Christ? Notice it is singular. The law of Christ doesn't say the laws of Christ. Some churches teach this to mean the laws of the preacher, the laws of the church and so on. Jesus said, "Come to me, all you who are heavy laden, and I will give you rest, for my yoke is easy and my burden is light" (Matthew 11:28–30). Come to me.

Jesus also said: "A new commandment I give you, that you love one another, even as I have loved you" (John 13:34). Now, how did Jesus love us?

"You shall call His name Jesus, for He shall save His people from their sins" (Matthew 1:21).

The Bible tells us in this verse that you shall call His name Jesus, for He shall save His people…and this next little word, this preposition, which is four letters long, is extremely important, from their sins. Jesus saves us from our sins. And if you're a person of grace, you will bear another person's trespass burden to save them from falling deeper into their sin.

Here's what that means. A friend intentionally crosses a boundary, or a parent, a child, a coworker, someone special to you, they trespass. You, as a grace person, are to gently seek to restore that person by walking with them and bearing their burden.

But this is what usually happens in churches. "Did you hear what so-and-so did?" "Oh, my goodness, I can't believe that. He should be punished."

I've discovered that when you have a group of people that looks at other people's trespasses and makes punitive judgments, you don't have a group that understands grace. You have a group that might be religious, prideful and/or spiritually arrogant, but you don't have a group that understands grace. Because when you understand grace, you're going to come alongside the person who is caught up in their trespass, and you're going to walk with them and bear their burden. Why? Because your goal is to be a physician, to heal them from their sins, not judge them because of their sins but to help heal them.

You say, "But pastor, here's my problem. There are some people who don't see what they're doing as sin. They don't see it as a trespass. In fact, they want to be left alone."

That's true. The Bible does speak to that. Proverbs 14:12 reads, "There is a way that seems right to a man. But its end is the way of death." You know what that means? That means anyone who crosses an appropriate fence and intentionally trespasses is in the wilderness of death. You go after them. They just might look at you and say, "I don't want you here. Get out of my life." To this you gently reply, "Hey, okay. I'll respect that. Listen, I love you. And when you're ready, I'll be there for you." You're like the doctor who never turns the sick patient away.

Then, perhaps one of these days, that person lost in his or her wilderness will think that he will find his own way out, but he won't. He'll be dying. And guess what? He'll issue a call. That's when you'll come alongside and bind up his wounds. You'll show the love of Christ and then help that person be delivered from their sins. This is what grace looks like, and this is what is missing in most of our churches.

Friends, this is why we as a grace people should make sure we're always paying attention to those in prison. We're always caring for those in sin. We're always exhibiting a spirit of gentleness to those who have fallen. We need to remind ourselves that we're just as capable of falling, so we're going to be diligent with our own lives because sick doctors can't help sick patients.

Let's stay on the lookout for any spirit of legalism or judgmentalism, any spirit of punitive rejection, any spirit that's not of grace. Let's get that out of our lives and truly live as image bearers of Christ.

Chapter Fourteen Discussion Questions

1. Helping people out of destructive behaviors is "physician work, not detective work." What does it mean to serve others as a physician versus a detective?
2. Graced people have eyes that see the needs of others. By contrast, what do eyes that haven't understood the loving grace of God tend to see?
3. Using the example of Emmanuel's ministry to ex-prison inmates, describe why corporate restoration ministry can be more effective than one-on-one ministry.
4. As people that have been captivated by the grace of God, why must we guard ourselves against a spirit of judgmentalism toward those that knowingly crossed that No Trespassing boundary?

Chapter Fifteen

"Eyes That Are Open to the Frailty of People"

Philippians 4:5
"Let your gentleness be evident to all."

When you became a Christian and gave your life to Jesus Christ, you didn't just wake up one morning smarter than you were the day before. You didn't become a Christian because you're wiser than the person you work beside or your neighbor across the street. The Bible says you began to follow Jesus because the God of all grace called you.

"The God of all grace who calls you."
(I Peter 5:10)

If He is your Heavenly Father and you've been born again into His family, He's called you into His kingdom and your purpose is to reflect Him in this world. In fact, the word Christian means little Christ.

And, if God is the God of all grace and Jesus said, 'He who has seen Me has seen the Father" (John 14:9), then we are to reflect the grace of God in this world. When you figure out what grace looks like, then you've figured out what God looks like, for He truly is the God of all grace.

Look at what the Bible says about Jesus. Jesus is "full of grace and truth" (John 1:14).

This is the only description we have in the Bible of the Lord Jesus Christ. The paintings that you see of Jesus today, a Caucasian with blonde or brown hair, simply are not accurate. He probably looked more Arab than He did Western European. The Bible does not tell us what Jesus physically looked like, but it does tell us that He was full of grace and truth.

Word order is important in Scripture. Grace comes first in the description of grace and truth, and the most important word always came first in ancient Biblical literature. Truth is second. You might be thinking, "What does that mean?" Simply this: if we're going to err, let's err on the side of having too much grace rather than too much truth, because truth without grace is cruel. Grace without truth is meaningless. There may be something meaningful to be said, but nobody will ever want to listen to our saying anything meaningful unless we're saying it in a gracious way.

In this chapter, we will see that the face of grace has eyes that are open to the frailty, or fragility if you will, of others. Graced people have:

Eyes that, Are Open to the Weaknesses of Others

I want to show you this from Philippians 4. The Apostle Paul is writing to Christians who live in the city of Philippi, thus, the title of his letter is Philippians. In this letter, he encourages followers of Jesus Christ to live a certain way, and one of the things that he says in Verse 5 of Chapter 4 is this. "Let your gentleness be known to all." Now, this word *gentleness* is a word that is often translated in English with the word *meek*, as in this example: Jesus said in Matthew 5:5, "Blessed are the meek." It's the same word used in Philippians which can be translated *gentle*.

Eyes That Are Open to the Frailty of People

"Blessed are the meek; they inherit the earth" (Matthew 5:5), or if we translate that word to *gentle*, "Blessed are the gentle, for they will inherit the earth." It's also the same word that Jesus used later on in the book of Matthew where He says of Himself, "I am gentle (meek) at heart" (Matthew 11:28).

Now, the question for us as we look at what the Scripture says about us is simply this, if God's people are gentle or meek, and Jesus said that He was, then what does that mean?

Have you ever seen a sculpted eggshell? It's the shell of an egg whose yolk has been taken out through a pinhole at the top of the egg, and then the shell was turned upside down. Next, an artist took a very sharp knife and he sculpted the shell. I can't even peel a hard-boiled egg without breaking it, but sculpting eggshells has become a fascinating art, particularly in Japan. In fact, they have created international guilds for those who sculpt eggshells, and it is tedious, disciplined work. Most of these sculptures are absolutely beautiful and they are also very expensive.

Now I want you to get in your mind sculpting an eggshell, and I propose to you that what the artist is doing is a description of meekness. Can you get that in your head? Here's what I mean: meekness does not mean weakness, but gentleness. Can you imagine how disciplined that sculptor is? How gentle he is with the eggshell? How focused he is? How persevering and longsuffering he is? It requires incredible strength in order to sculpt an eggshell. That's the very description of what it means to be meek.

Meekness is not weakness. Meekness or gentleness is strength that is under control.

As you go through life, you're living in a culture and a world that doesn't understand gentleness. It's all about aggressiveness. It's all about inserting oneself into an environment so that change occurs.

"I'm the top dog" is the mentality. You work for me. I will make you do what I want you to do. That's not controlled strength, that's uncontrolled strength, and God's people are not to exhibit that at all.

When my boys were little, I took them to karate lessons. Sadly, it didn't last long. It was a lot of fun, but because of lack of time on my part and the loss of interest on theirs, we stopped going. We did manage to go long enough that I could learn a couple of things from the karate teacher.

He said, "You can always tell who the guys are who can win the fight, because they're under control. They're gentle. They're quiet. It's the insecure guys who insert themselves, who with bravado say all kinds of things to intimidate." He said, "Those are the guys who aren't going to win."

When we began to follow Jesus Christ, He called us to come under control. He gave us the grace to do this because this is who He is. He wants us to have strength but to keep it under wraps. You might think, "I don't understand what you mean." Well, let me make it clear. What I mean is if somebody wrongs you, you keep your mouth from cursing them. If somebody does something to you that hurts you, wounds you, you're strong enough by the power of who you are in Christ to go ahead and maintain strength under control. You might be saying, "I can't." Yes, you can. Let me show you how.

First, to be meek is to know your Heavenly Papa. I'm using the word Papa rather than Father intentionally because I think it's the more appropriate Biblical word. I got it from my friend William Paul Young, who wrote the book The Shack. In that book, Paul calls God the Father, Papa, because the word Papa comes closer to the Greek word *Abba*, meaning an affectionate, dependent relationship with one's father. That was used in Jesus' day in terms of God. Abba Father is what followers of Jesus cried out. And Abba means Papa, Daddy. When you know your Daddy, your Heavenly Papa, you understand that He's got your back.

You see, when you find yourself in a situation that's out of control, you've just got to remember your Papa. He's promised you that He will work all things together for your good. (Romans 8:28) When you think you need something and you get out of control in order to get it from people, you've forgotten your Papa, Who has promised you that He will provide for your every need. God's people are to be gentle. We're to be meek.

To be meek is to understand your earthly purpose. Very few people in this world are gentle, but followers of Jesus are to be that way. This gentleness, this meekness doesn't mean weakness. It means strength under control. But there is an even easier way of saying it. Meekness simply means a *lack of meanness*.

We pastors gather each Sunday morning and we pray that people who come to our worship services will leave encouraged. I've been a pastor for a long time now, and I understand that often when we come to church, we might have just had a rip-roaring fight with the people we love. There may have been yelling and maybe even cursing and fighting and so on. But then a handful of minutes later, you listen to a talk about how people who follow Christ, graced people, are to be gentle. It hurts. It cuts.

So, let me show you a couple of things that might encourage us. The Greek word that is translated gentle or meek is the word *epieikes*, and it is used three times in the New Testament in different places. It helps to know the places that it's used so that we understand how gentleness works. First, it is used in 1 Timothy 3:3 to describe the character of a pastor. In other words, if you're ever called into the pastorate, you must display the character of gentleness.

The Face of Grace

There's a well-known pastor in Chicago, I won't mention his name, but it's a matter of public record so I'm not saying anything that is confidential. He was removed from his church by the elders of his church because he was really harsh toward the members of his congregation, incredibly so. He would yell at people. He was caught on tape cursing members. One woman in his church, a newspaper reporter, went privately to try to confront some of the meanness. She got absolutely nowhere, so she wrote a blog about it and the pastor decided to sue that woman. Then Christianity Today, the leading magazine for evangelical Christians in the United States, allowed this pastor to run a guest editorial slamming the woman as "unchristian" for what she had said about him and his ministry. It's one of the worst examples of bullying I've seen in a long time.

Just this week, the managing editor of Christianity Today got into a dialogue with me, and one of the things that was discussed is that anytime you have a church, whether it's Emmanuel Enid, or one like this church in Chicago, a parish, a synagogue, the leader of people who assemble in the name of Christ is to be gentle. And if he's not, he's disqualified himself from pastoral ministry because the Chief Shepherd is gentle at heart, and every undershepherd is to have that same kind of character.

The second place this word is used is in James 3:17 where it describes wisdom, wisdom which is *epieikes*, meaning gentle. You know what this means? You know who the people are that you should be getting advice from? It's from people with a gentle heart. I can prove this to you instantly. How many of you remember as kids going to your grandparents? Do you remember spending time with them, talking about things with them? What was it that drew you to them? Most of the time your grandparents, those with silver hair would speak to you gently.

Eyes That Are Open to the Frailty of People

It's one of the reasons why in the New Testament, the Scripture says those who are elders in the church are to be leaders of the assembly. Now, modern evangelicals totally mess up that word, elder. They assign some mystical spiritual authority to an office and they address that person with the title, an elder. No. An elder is that silver-haired man or woman who is wise and gentle.

The best illustration I can give of that is our former chairperson of the leadership team here at Emmanuel. Her name was Gail Hackett. She came to us from a sister church and sadly, she died a couple of years ago. What a wise woman, what a gentle soul. You and I should be going to people for wisdom who have this gentleness of character.

You might ask, "Well, pastor, does that rule out a young man from being able to be meek?"

No, not at all. But before you ever put a young man or woman in a position of leadership, you should test his or her character in terms of gentleness, because the third place this word is used in the New Testament is in Titus 3:2. The Bible says that Paul, writing a letter to young Titus, who was a young pastor says, "Titus, show gentleness above all, make that part of your life and teach others around you how to be meek." *Epieikes* is the word that he uses, and in this case it's also to be taught to others. Why is this important? Well, let me just become very personal with you from my own life. There are times when I am less than gentle, when I am not meek, when my strength is uncontrolled. Let me tell you what uncontrolled strength reveals in me.

It reveals insecurity. When my ability to speak, or when my logic or the strength that God has gifted me with is not under control, when it's out of control and I get forceful, domineering and demanding, something's wrong in me. There's an insecurity I'm revealing. Like what, you ask? Well, let's say that someone has said something about me and I don't like what was said. It makes me feel devalued. It makes me feel as if I haven't done well enough.

This shows that I've forgotten a couple of things. Number one, nobody should have the control over how I feel except my Papa, Who has told me that even if I'm imperfect, He always embraces me. Even if I'm running and hiding, He always pursues and seeks me. Even when I don't measure up, He accepts me. My uncontrolled strength reveals to you some insecurity in my own life, and I've taken my eyes off of my Papa and put them on my environment.

So, this show of uncontrolled strength is not my character. It's not who I am because the God of all grace has adopted me into His family. He has indwelled me and He has called me to reflect Him in a world that is lost. So, when I start acting like the world and not my Papa, I'm revealing to you something that is contrary to the character the grace of God has given me.

You could say, "How can that happen? You are who you are." Well, let me show you something. Before I came to know Christ, I had a pattern in my life, a pattern that I lived by. My wife knows what that pattern was. I would always help the underdog and step up to the big dog, face him down, and lift up the underdog. I think it came from the experience of being bullied in the 4th grade, and the emotions that I felt have been forever seared into the memory bank of my mind. It's just there. I successfully resisted him, so I understand the pain of being bullied by someone bigger, more powerful, with more authority. Because of that, I will come to the aid of the underdog. But I have to be careful, because sometimes I get into the flesh and I end up taking the position of uncontrolled strength. That's not good. That's not grace at work, that's my flesh.

Eyes That Are Open to the Frailty of People

Here's another illustration. Let's say we had a big wooden barrel, a cask of wine, and right next to it was an empty container. Let's say that this wine barrel was made in the old days, in the ancient days of Christ. Let's say that you and I were able to pick up this container of wine and pour the wine into the empty container. Then we set the now emptied barrel, which formerly had wine in it, onto the ground and filled it with fresh spring water all the way to the top. You and I got a cup and we dipped that cup into the spring water, then we walked away with our drink. We could still smell the wine. We could still taste the wine. Why? Because all that's happened is something new has been put into the container, but the container hasn't changed and it still has the residue of what used to be in it, what used to fill it.

When you came to faith in Jesus Christ, something new was given to you, a new heart, but the container didn't change. The residue of what filled you before remains. Some of you have experiences of abuse when you were young. Some of you carry incredible pain that you cannot get out of your mind. Here's the deal. Even though you're a new person and grace means that you're gentle, every now and then you and I slip into the old flesh and we act like what we used to be, domineering, controlling, angry, needy, and so on.

When that happens, uncontrolled strength just needs your confession.

The people you love who experience your meanness that is contrary to your character, you just ask for their forgiveness. That's all. "Hey, sweetheart. Gosh, I'm so sorry. What I said to you, how I yelled at you. Listen. That's not who God has made me. Will you forgive me? I fell back into that old pattern of the way I used to live."

It's that simple. I remember a few years ago I asked the question, how many times do you think I apologize to the people I love? I came to the conclusion and I publicly confessed, probably about seven times a day seeking forgiveness, apologizing, saying, I'm sorry, and so on.

A person came up to me after that service and said, "Are you kidding me? Seven times a day on average? I've been a Christian (the person named the number of years) and I'm not sure I've ever sought forgiveness of anything I've ever done." And as we talked, you know what we discovered? We discovered that to this person, acknowledging doing something wrong was acknowledging weakness. I was able to show him that's not true at all. Acknowledging that you've done something wrong and taking responsibility for it is meekness. It's strength under control.

Meekness does not mean being speechless. It doesn't imply weakness. Meekness does mean a lack of meanness, but meekness doesn't mean remaining speechless. If you see something that is wrong, it doesn't mean that you have to remain quiet. You speak the truth. You speak the truth, but you do so in love. You're full of grace first, then truth, because even if it's meaningful, nobody will ever listen to what we say until they catch the grace with which we say it.

You might ask, "But Pastor, what happens if I'm really wounded or hurt?"

To this I would reply with God's Word: "Do not take revenge; leave room for God's just wrath. For it is written: 'It is mine to avenge; I will repay,' says the Lord" (Romans 12:19).

Have you been called by Christ? Are you in His family? Are you in His Kingdom? I guarantee you, the world does not understand this. The ways of the world are defined by force. It's all meanness. It's all, "I'll get you to do what I want you to do. I'll dominate and control you." But for the followers of Jesus, His call is to have eyes that see the frailty of people. His way is to take the eggshell, and with strength under control, carve a story called your life that is portrayed by gentleness and meekness. This is what grace looks like, and if it's not present in our lives, maybe…just maybe…the God of all grace is lovingly saying to us, "Trust Me more than you do anything else."

Chapter Fifteen Discussion Questions

1. When Jesus is described as being "full of grace and truth", why is "grace" mentioned first and "truth" second?
2. What does uncontrolled strength reveal about our inner state?
3. How can gentleness or meekness (strength under control) be more effective than uncontrolled strength?

Section IV

Ears That Hear

Chapter Sixteen

"Ears That Hear the Word of Christ"

Matthew 17:1-8
"This is my beloved Son, with whom I am well-pleased, Listen to Him!."

The Bible tells us that Jesus was a man full of grace and truth. And, the word Christian means *little Christ*, so when someone comes across our path, we are as a "little Christ" to them. We are to be a people full of grace and truth. What does that mean? Simply, we should look and act like Jesus. He gave us a new birth. He is our Father, our spiritual Father.

Recently, one of our pastors showed me a picture of his son, and beside that picture was a picture of himself taken 25 years ago. You couldn't tell them apart because they looked like they were clones. That comes as no surprise, because we usually expect a son to look like his father.

Do you look like Christ? Well, I want to show you that if I claim to be a follower of Jesus, and if I say to you I am a Christian, that simply means that among other things I should have

---

Ears that,

Hear the Word of Christ

Grace means you listen to Jesus. That's what it looks like, and I'll show you this from the Scriptures. If you've ever read the Bible beginning in Genesis and through the Old Testament, what is the concept of God that you've come away with? Let me ask another question. When you read what we call the Old Testament, from Genesis to Malachi, what do you come away with about yourself?

If you're like the average person, you read the Old Testament and you think God is angry. God sent a flood to wipe out the entire world, save one family. God lost His patience with His chosen people as they complained during 40 years of wandering in the wilderness. God punished Israel (His chosen) when they would forget Him and serve the gods of the land that He gave them in Canaan.

You read all this and conclude that He's probably upset with you, too. You might already be a lost cause, and you're never going to be able to please Him. You can come away a little bit like, Why don't you just stay away, God, mind Your own business and I'll live my life. Typically, we suffer a disconnect when we read the Old Testament because we don't like the concept of God that is delivered there. May I propose to you that if that's what you come away with when you read the Old Testament, you've possibly misread it.

Now I will admit to you, as the great theologian Emil Kraeling once said, "The correct use of the Old Testament is the master problem of theology." What that means is you've got to figure out what to do with the Old Testament before you have any idea of who God is, so I'd like to help you. I want to show you that the Old Testament is not the foundation that you build your home on in terms of your faith, and then live in. It is the foundation of your faith, but it's not your home.

Here's what I mean by that. If you read the Old Testament and you come across commandments and laws and prohibitions and dietary restrictions and everything like that, and you say, "Oh my, that wears me out, but if I don't do this, then God's not going to be happy..." If this is what you think when you read all the Sabbatarian laws, and all the laws and regulations of that type, that may mean that you've missed God. You've missed the Old Testament.

You say, "What do you mean?"

Well, listen to Jesus. He was speaking to some religious people in His day that were experts in what we call the Old Testament. They only knew it as the Scriptures. They were lawyers that were experts in the Law. Yet, listen to what Jesus said to the Pharisees: "The Scriptures" (meaning the Old Testament) "testify of Me. But you are unwilling to come to Me to have life" (John 5:39-40).

Do you hear what Jesus is saying? The Old Testament is about Him. It would be as if I were to give you my diary and I said, "Read this," and you would say, "What is it?" I would say to you, "These are writings about me."

By the way, after His resurrection, walking to a little community called Emmaus, there were two men walking beside him. Listen to what Jesus said to them.

"And beginning with Moses and all the prophets, Jesus explained to them what was said in all the Scriptures concerning Himself" (Luke 24:27).

Beginning with Moses (that's the first five books of the Old Testament), and the Prophets (that's the rest of the books of the Old Testament and the writings), Jesus explained to these two men all that was said in all the Scriptures concerning Himself.

What? You may even say to me, "Pastor, I've read the Old Testament and I've never come across the name of Jesus." Well, let me show you how everything in the Old Testament is the foundation of your faith. You're not to live in it, but you are to see what the Old Testament is about, and it's about Jesus Christ.

Let's take the moon as an example. Did you realize that the Jews in the Old Testament kept time by the moon? Did you know that?

I'm guessing probably not. In fact, you have never read about January, February, March, April, May, June, or July in the Old Testament, because they didn't follow those dates or months. They used a calendar based upon the moon.

We've got a lot of farmers in our community and I envy those guys. They're out there on the farms without the illumination of the city lights. They have the stars and the moon with complete darkness, and they know what the entire night sky looks like. I envy them.

The Jews back in the day with no streetlights kept time by the moon. They didn't have watches, phones, or calendars. You know what they did when they saw a new moon? Trumpets were blown in Jerusalem, and the people celebrated with a feast because a new month had begun. We read about the Feast of the New Moon in Colossians 2:16. By the way, the word *month* comes from the word moon. A month lasted about twenty-nine and a half days. The Jews would watch the cycles of the moon from a new moon to a full moon to a waning moon. Halfway through the lunar month when the moon was full, it was called the Ides. We get our word *divide* from the word *Ides*, the Ides of March, the middle of March and so on.

You say, why is that important? July the Fourth, Easter, Christmas, and Labor Day are some of our holidays in America, but when you read the Old Testament, it's all about the holidays of the Jews. They call them holy days, which is where we get the word *holiday*. You know how many holidays the Jews had in the Old Testament? They had seven, and all were based on the lunar calendar.

In fact, in spring, in the month of Abib, which was the first lunar month of Israel corresponding roughly to our solar month of March or April, they had three spring festivals: Passover, Unleavened Bread, and the Feast of First Fruits. Fifty days after Passover they celebrated Pentecost in the middle of the summer. Then in the fall they had another three festivals: the Feast of Trumpets (Rosh Hashanah), the Feast of Atonement (Yom Kippur), and the Feast of Tabernacles.

Here's what's fascinating. When you read the Old Testament, you read about these holidays. Why did they celebrate these? Because God told them to. In fact, He not only told them to, He set the calendar. For example, in Exodus, He said to the Jews, "This month (meaning the first month Abib) is to be the first month of your year" (Exodus 12:2). The holiday called Passover is what the Jews to this day celebrate, and they still follow their religious calendar based on the moon. We in the West follow the calendar where our year is based on the sun, specifically, the earth's revolution around the sun. But guess what? When we celebrate Easter, the resurrection of Christ, it just so happens that we do so on the first Sunday after the first spring full moon, which makes it a lunar calendar holiday.

Back to the Passover celebration, do you know what the Jews did? Every year they went to Jerusalem, and they would bring their lambs to celebrate what God had done as recorded in the Book of Exodus in delivering his people out of Egypt. You recall the story.

On that first Passover night, fifteen hundred years before Christ even came to earth, God's people were in bondage in the land of Egypt. The Pharaoh of Egypt had made them slaves and demanded they make bricks. Make bricks, make more bricks. They were building the pyramids. Do more. Work harder. And the Jews were worn out. They were in pain, and they cried out to Yahweh for deliverance.

God sent them a man by the name of Moses. Remember the story. Moses was their deliverer. God sent ten plagues. Nowadays every year at Passover, ABC TV runs the story of Moses starring Charlton Heston. We watch what the Jews did; they took a lamb that first Passover night and they killed it. Then they took the blood of that lamb and spread it on the doorpost of their home at the top, the threshold, and on the sides of their door because Moses told them to. God had said, "Tonight, I'm going through the land. Everywhere I see the blood, I will pass over you. But where there is no blood, there will be death." You can read the full story in Exodus 12.

By the way, where the Jews put the blood on that door is prophetic because they put it in the exact places where Jesus Christ's blood was found on the cross: the crown of thorns on his head. The nails in his hands and the nails in his feet, with his feet on top of each other.

So that night, the Jews left Egypt because the firstborn of the Egyptians were all killed. There was no blood applied to the doorposts of the Egyptians' homes. And as they were wailing and weeping, the Jews fled and went to the promised land, the land of Israel.

From that time forward, the Jews every year would return to Jerusalem after Solomon built the temple and celebrate the Passover with the lamb that they brought to Yahweh.

"Every year Jesus' parents went to Jerusalem for the Festival of the Passover. When he was twelve years old, they went up to the festival, according to the custom" (Luke 2:41-42). Even Jesus, a good Jewish boy did this every year. Jesus' parents went to Jerusalem for the festival of the Passover, and when he was twelve years old they went up to the festival according to the custom.

When you read about the Passover in the Old Testament, do you think about Jesus Christ? Here's what Jesus said during his ministry. "Do not think that I have come to abolish the Law or the prophets." Do you see that phrase again? Moses and Elijah, the Law and the prophets. "Don't think that I've come to destroy the Law and the prophets. I have come to fulfill them." (Matthew 5:17)

What does that mean? Do you know why God established the calendar in the Old Testament? Do you know why He told the Jews to celebrate their seven holy days? It's because it's all about Jesus

Ears That Hear the Words of Christ

Christ. On Passover day, nineteen hundred and ninety years ago, Abib 14, A.D. 30 as we reckon time, Jesus Christ died at the age of 33 on Passover day at 3 o'clock in the afternoon. As all the Jewish people were slaying their lambs to celebrate Passover and God's deliverance by the blood, Jesus Christ, the Lamb of God, shed His blood for you and for me.

When the soldiers came around to take Jesus down from the cross, you remember it says that they were going to break his legs because they needed Him off the cross. They needed Jesus off the cross because the end of the day was approaching, and Passover was about to begin. The evening of Passover day is a new day for the Jews. The way they reckoned time was that a new day began at 6:00 p.m., although in Western thinking it's just the evening of the day when the lamb was killed. The fathers would kill the lambs that they had brought to Jerusalem for their families. Then in their tents that they had pitched they would basically roast the lamb, and afterward they'd eat what's called the Passover meal.

The soldiers needed Jesus off the cross because the religious people had said, "We don't want people hanging on the cross when we eat the Passover meal." So, they went around to break his legs and hurry up His death, but he was already dead. So, they took Him off the cross and they put Him in the tomb before sunset, then all the people went to their homes to eat the Passover.

And you know what the Passover meal was called? It's called Unleavened Bread. It was the beginning of a week-long celebration called the Feast of Unleavened Bread. During that whole week you had to eat bread that was made without yeast. In fact, Jewish women would be in their little tents or their huts or their paid rooms, and they would sweep away the leaven. What does leaven represent in the Old Testament? It's a picture of sin. Here at this Passover, Jesus Christ is in the

The Face of Grace

tomb, sweeping away our sins. During the Feast of Unleavened Bread, He is fulfilling the Law.

During the week of Passover, the third festival Israel celebrated was the Feast of First Fruits. All Jewish families that came to Jerusalem to celebrate Passover were required to by law. The men would go into their fields in the early spring when just a few grains had budded, and they would take a sheaf of those first fruits and take it to Jerusalem. Farmers know that most of the grain crops are harvested during the summer, but in the spring they would bring their first fruits. Then during Passover week on the day after the regular Sabbath, which was Saturday, making that day our Sunday, all the Jewish men would take their sheaf of first fruits and go to the temple courtyard where they would wave it. This is what they would pray: "Yahweh, as you have blessed the first fruits of my farm, will you please bless the full harvest."

It was on that very morning that Jesus Christ rose from the grave. This helps us understand the Apostle Paul in First Corinthians 15, when speaking of the resurrection he says, "Christ is the first fruits of resurrection guaranteeing the full harvest."

Any of you who follow Jesus Christ will be raised from the dead to live forever because Jesus Christ is fulfilling the law in your place. Take Pentecost. On the Festival of Pentecost, the Holy Spirit came to indwell the followers of Jesus. I could go on to the fall festivals such as the Festival of Trumpets, where the old covenant was destroyed in the judgment of Christ that He predicted in Matthew 24, fulfilled in September of A.D. 70.

My point to you is this: when you think about the cross today and you think about the empty tomb, it's simply a fulfillment of the Old Testament.

You say, "Pastor, but why does that even make any difference?" I'll tell you why. Because if you pick up the Old Testament and you try to live *in* it and you look and see an angry God whom you will never please, you see commandments and restrictions and all the Sabbath laws and you think, "Oh, I just can't do it. I just can't do it." Truth is, you are not called to do it. If you read the Old Testament and you don't see Jesus in it, you're misreading it. Jesus came to fulfill the law, and then abolish it. He came to abolish the law and establish a new agreement with the entire world.

"By calling this covenant 'new,' He has made the first one obsolete; and what is obsolete and outdated will soon disappear" (Hebrews 8:13).

So, in A.D. 70, when God in judgment destroyed the temple and all the official sacrifices that went with it, and made Jerusalem desolate, it was the inauguration of a new kingdom. Now, let's look at this agreement God has made with the world.

First, there's a *new law*, given by the Law-giver Jesus, which means if you're looking to Moses for the way to live, you're missing Jesus. He's the new Law-Giver. You know what His law is? It's called the Royal Law of Love.

Simply put, if you want to know what a Christian looks like, look at what Jesus said. "A new commandment I give to you, that you love one another as I have loved you" (John 13:34). James calls this the royal law. It's that simple.

You say, "But I need restrictions. I need covenants. I need laws. I need things that are posted that say, 'Don't do this and don't do that.'" Hey, wait a second. You can't love your wife and be unfaithful to her. You can't love your neighbor and steal his lawn mower. You can't love the man who slanders you and then hate him. It's the only law you need.

We have in this new agreement a *new method*. We worship the Lord in spirit and in truth. We don't need the rituals. We don't even need a priest or a pastor. We worship our Creator in spirit and in truth.

In this new agreement, we have a new place. You are the temple of the living God. (I Corinthians 3:16) Wherever you go, God is. In the Old Testament, you had to go to Jerusalem to see the habitation of Yahweh. Now all you have to do is go wherever Yahweh's kids are. See, this is what's so radically new about this new agreement God has inaugurated with the world.

We have a *new mission* as well. Back in the Old Testament it was always "Come and See." Come and see our pageantry, come and see our high priest, come and see our sacrifices. Come and see us in Jerusalem. Come and see the temple. But not anymore. Now it's go and tell. We are to go and tell that poor person of the riches of God's grace. We are to go and tell that lonely person that the Father has promised never to leave nor forsake anyone who embraces His Son. We are to go and tell that person who thinks there is no purpose in life that the Father will give purpose to anyone who listens to His Son.

In this new agreement, there's a *new expectation*.

You read the promises of God in the Old Testament, and most all of them are all conditional. If you, then I. God says, "If you obey me, then I will bless you. But if you turn away from me, (this was the law) then other nations will come in and destroy your crops and take your family captive and put you in prison as well" (Deuteronomy 28). You say, "Wow!"

By the way, the Old Testament is nothing but a record of Israel's failure to keep the Law. Why? Why did Israel fail? Because the Law is a schoolmaster that takes every human being by the hand. And Israel was a model of this for us, to lead us to the true Israel. The Law says don't, don't, don't, don't, and meanwhile, the school child is fighting against the Law. Then finally, the Law takes us to Christ, and Christ says, "Alright, now you've fought long enough. I'm your Teacher. Love people like I love you." Wow!

In this new agreement there is a *new people*–all nations and peoples. As a new people in the Old Testament, it's the Jews. Every now and then you could have other people from other nations join, but they had to go through the rituals. Not anymore. The new agreement is a message to the entire world, for all peoples.

In Matthew Chapter 17, Jesus takes Peter, James, and John his brother, and leads them up on a high mountain by themselves. Now, this mountain is the mount we call Tabor. It's a round mountain and there is a monastery at the top today. But back in Jesus' day it was round and barren. And the three followers of Jesus, people like you and me, went with Him.

Matthew 17:2: "And He was transfigured before them, and His face shone like the sun, and His garments became as white as light."

Scripture tells us that Jesus was transfigured before them. That means he changed in appearance; his face shown like the sun. His garments became white as light. And behold, Moses and Elijah appeared and were talking to Jesus.

Matthew 17:4, "Peter said to Jesus, 'Lord, it is good for us to be here; if You wish, I will make three tabernacles here, one for You, and one for Moses, and one for Elijah.'"

That sounds like something I would say. I would be so excited that now I might get to converse with Elijah and Moses. "Let's talk." Moses lived fifteen hundred years before this time. Elijah, the chief of prophets, appeared on this mountain. They could tell me so much! Moses was the Law giver. Elijah was the great prophet of old. All the writings of the Old Testament, Moses and Elijah represented them all.

Do you remember what Jesus said to those two men on the road to Emmaus? "And beginning with Moses and all the prophets, Jesus explained to them what was said in all the Scriptures concerning Himself" (Luke 24:27).

"I want to talk to these guys." Peter seems to say. And amazingly, as Peter was still speaking asking if he could build three tabernacles, a bright cloud overshadowed them and behold, the voice out of the clouds said, and this is God speaking. "This is my beloved Son, with whom I am well pleased. Listen to Him" (Matthew 17:5).

When the disciples heard this, they fell down to the ground and they were terrified. And Jesus came to them and touched them and said, "Get up and do not be afraid" and lifting up their eyes they saw no one except Jesus Himself alone" (Matthew 17:6–8).

Here's just a simple word of encouragement. What God actually said to the disciples in their own language, and I'll translate it in English, was this. "This is my beloved Son in whom I am well pleased. Hear Him." *Acoute Auton* is translated hear Him. We get our English word acoustics from the Greek word *acoute*, and *auton* is the preposition for him. Hear Him.

You might ask, "What does that mean?" Simply this. Our Christian life can be boiled down to something very simple. We are not to worry about any religious laws or ceremonies. We are not to worry about how religious we are in the eyes of other people. No, no. A graced person hears Jesus Christ.

I'll give you three ways to hear Jesus. Number one, His words. Let's just make it simple. You open up the Scriptures, get you a red-letter edition of the Bible and just read the words of Jesus Christ. Hear him. *Acoute Auton!*

You don't have to be Pastor Wade. Man, I read the Old Testament. I'm reading it in its native language. I listen to history. I listen to

Ears That Hear the Words of Christ

Julius Caesar and his life in my head as I go to sleep. I love that kind of reading, hearing, and learning. You don't have to be the way I am, doing so much.

Just read His Word and listen! Listen to Jesus Christ. What is Jesus saying to you as you read His words from the Scriptures?

Another way we hear Jesus is by His Spirit. We follow Jesus. His Spirit is in us because His Spirit has taken up residence within us believers. Listen to His Spirit, an impression within as you are reading His Word and praying. You ask, "But how do I know it's the Spirit of God?" Oh, there's usually a pretty easy way. First, the Spirit within you will never contradict the words of your Master. And second, what you feel impressed within you as a follower of Jesus is usually contrary to what the world is telling you to do.

And a third way to hear Jesus is through His people. I tell you, if your best friends are people who don't know Jesus, it could be like the blind leading the blind. If you want to know how to live life, get around people who know Jesus.

Here's an example that illustrates this truth. I recently visited the father of one of our members who had just turned 100. George is an amazing man. For a period of time, for several years, he was a shepherd. The real thing! He literally watched over 150 to 200 sheep.

George told me, "Wade, I've got to tell you something. Don't let anybody tell you anything differently. When a shepherd goes out into the fields and calls his sheep, they all come running. But Wade, you could go out into a field, and you could call my sheep and none would come, but when my sheep hear my voice, they come."

I said, "George, wait. All of them? All the time?"

He said, "Well, to be honest with you, ninety-eight percent of the time they all come, but about two percent of the time when my voice is heard, a couple of them won't come."

I said, "George, what do you do then?"

He said, "Let me introduce you to my sheep dog." He then showed me a picture of his sheep dog and said, "I just let the dog loose. And as soon as the sheep see the dog coming, they come running to the shepherd."

How do you know you're a Christian? What does it mean to be full of grace? Forget the religion that is based on ceremony. Forget this idea of smoke and priests and pronouncements and absolution based upon religious ritual. That's an old covenant that has disappeared.

Acuete Auton! Hear Him.

Perhaps you're really struggling with some decisions in life these days. Maybe you're thinking about doing something, and I mean, it's a battle, it's a struggle. You don't know where to go. You don't know what to do. You don't know who to listen to.

Hear Him! And I promise you, the Chief Shepherd will never lead you astray. The essence of being a "little Christ", a follower of Jesus, is to be a person who hears. May it be so in our lives.

Chapter Sixteen Discussion Questions

1. What would your concept of God be, if all you had to go by were the commandments, laws and statutes of the Old Testament?
2. How does Jesus change our concept of God?
3. What are three ways that we can "hear Jesus"?
4. How can we know for sure that what we are hearing is truly from Him, and not from a false source or an imposter?

Chapter Seventeen

"Ears That Are Deaf to the Lies of this World"

John 8:42-44
"He (the devil) is a liar and the father of lies."

I have been asking the question, what does grace look like? You know what I look like because of my face. I know what you look like because of your face. We say we believe in grace, but what does grace look like? We've been looking at the mind of grace, the mouth of grace, and the eyes of grace. Now we've come to the ears of grace.

What do graced people hear?

Now, I need to be clear about something before we examine grace any further. If you are an employer, you're going to read about grace and you'll make a mistake if you think that I'm saying you should adopt this as an employer. No, that's not what I'm saying. You have people who work for you under contract. Employers and employees who hear and read the message of grace make a mistake if they try to apply the principles of grace to a work contract. Don't ever confuse employment contracts with the principle of grace.

What we're going to look at is how we relate to one another in personal relationships. Set aside all contracts, and by the way, I would even say this includes a marriage contract, because when you sign a marriage contract, there are things that you pledge and vow to do. What's more, sometimes you have to fulfill the contract, or consequences are implemented when the contract is broken. Set aside all contracts for now and let's look at our personal relationships with one another, people created in the image of God. We are to be people filled with grace.

God is the God of all grace. He has adopted us into His family. He has redeemed us and He has saved us. Jesus was a man full of grace and truth. We're followers of Jesus, so we're to be full of grace and truth in our personal relationships.

Now let's just be candid and honest, okay? Let me share something about my life. I publicly repent of having gone out in the sun without sunscreen when I was young. Whether it was playing ball, whether it was playing golf or going to the beach, I didn't wear sunscreen. I didn't think I needed it anytime I went outside.

Well, recently they removed a cancer off of my shoulder, and I have a big scar on it. Then the doctor put my face underneath a light and she said, "Oh, you also need to have treatment on your face." So, for several weeks I received chemical treatment, a little bit like a topical chemotherapy treatment on my face. I think some of you may have had it too. It's called Fluorouracil and I'm telling you, it made me miserable, uncomfortable. It was painful. My lips were blistered. My eyes did not do well, and boy, you should have seen my face. Oh, my word. I was pock-marked. I was scarred. I had red sores covering my face.

The doctor said that all this misery was *good*, because it was a sign I was healing. No one was able to see the sores or the redness on my face because I was given a medicine that was tinted to cover it up. Now, my wife has seen my untreated face and she doesn't really care. She loves me and exhibits that all the time. Rachelle knew what I really looked like, and it made no difference to her.

I share this story because the fact of the matter is, any time we come to church we all want to cover our blemishes. We don't want people to know what is really going on in our lives. There's really not anything necessarily wrong with that because that's the way the world operates. But there are occasions when we will get to know people and we will see them with all of their blemishes, all of their pockmarks, all of their scars. I want to show you this morning how we are to treat them.

By the way, being in the position that I'm in, I know things about people that are unknown to others, because they call me when their life has been scarred. Recently, within a 24-hour period I had four calls from people affiliated with our church. I can't say they attend regularly, but they consider Emmanuel Enid their home church. Two of them called me just broken, crying, asking to get together with me. You know why they're weeping? It's because they've just looked at themselves in the mirror and they've seen the scars, and probably what's even worse is everybody else now knows what they really look like. Two of them saw their crimes printed on the front page of the local paper, and they were shattered because now everybody knows about them, their faults, their scars, their crimes.

How do we relate to them? I'm not asking this question from the standpoint of a professional relationship such as their teacher or their employer. How do we as followers of Jesus, how do we personally relate to them? I would propose to you that we relate to them the exact same way my wife did with me when she saw my face for what it really was with all its redness and scars. She saw me as I really was, and its damaged condition made no difference to her. This is how grace views others, and this is how graced people relate.

Now, I want to show you that if we are followers of Jesus, full of grace, we have:

Ears that,
Are Deaf to the Lies of this World

The Face of Grace

and we listen to the truth. That's who we are. That is grace.

Applying this to the face of grace, that's the kind of ears that Jesus tells us we are to have. In the Book of John, Chapter 8, Jesus is in conversation with Jewish people who are extremely religious. Jesus basically tells them in Verse 41, "If you know God, you will continue in my words." The Jews respond to Him, saying, "What? Wait, wait, wait a minute. What do you mean, *if* we know God? All of us know God. We are children of Abraham. We are Jews." It would be like one of us saying, "What do you mean, '*Am* I a Christian?' Of course, I'm a Christian. I go to church. I'm religious."

Well, Jesus responds to them in John 8:42: "If God were your Father, you would love Me, for I proceeded forth and have come from God, for I have not come on My own initiative, but He sent Me." He then says in Verse 43, "Why do you not understand what I am saying? Is it because you cannot hear My word?" The answer is, of course, yes.

[44a] "You are of your father the devil, and you want to do the desires of your father. He was a murderer from the beginning and does not stand in the truth because there is no truth in him."

[44b] "When he speaks a lie, he speaks from his own nature, for he is a liar and the father of lies."

If you want to know what grace looks like, it's the grace that indwells followers of Jesus. If you want to know what a real Christian is, it's one who is taken out from the family of lies and adopted into the family of truth. It's a person who grows deaf to the lies of their former father, the devil, and then begins to listen to the truth of their new Father, the Lord Jesus Christ.

In this text Jesus says, "If God is your father, you will love me." You will love Jesus. Let's stop a minute and think about that. You attend church on Sunday mornings. Other people are out at the lake

Ears That Are Deaf to the Lies of this World

on a beautiful day. Maybe they are playing golf. They're playing baseball. You come to a corporate worship service, yet your redemption does not require that. Your salvation, the favor of God does not demand that you attend church. Oh no, not at all. But you still choose to attend. Wow. You have an appetite for the Lord Jesus. You love Him.

You and I need to be careful, though. Oftentimes we will judge our love for the Lord Jesus by how faithful we are in things like attending church or obeying Him in general. There may be some reading this that have really struggled about their walk with Christ because some things that took place in their life have caused them unbelievable embarrassment. They're almost ashamed to even talk about them. If you are one who has experienced this, you may be questioning your love for Jesus. Don't! It's a lie. It's a lie of your former father when he whispers in your ear, "Hey, listen, if you really knew God, you'd love Jesus better than you are." No, that's not true. That's a lie from the father of lies. You already love Jesus. You do. And by the way, more importantly, Jesus knows you do.

Let me show you what I mean. Do you remember Peter? Peter, the disciple who swore allegiance to Christ in the garden of Gethsemane. Peter, who took out a sword and even chopped off an ear of a servant and resisted those who came to arrest Jesus. Later that night, Peter was hanging out in front of a charcoal fire. The Bible specifically says it's a charcoal fire. John 18:18 in the English Standard Version: "Now the servants and officers had made a charcoal fire, because it was cold, and they were standing and warming themselves. Peter also was with them, warming himself." Pay attention to that. It's not a fire made of wood. It's a fire made of charcoal. This would mean it had a distinct smell, like when you grill hamburgers over charcoal; you can smell it throughout your neighborhood.

The Face of Grace

It was there, before that charcoal fire that a young girl said to Peter, "I know you. You know Jesus, you're a follower of Jesus. You're one of his disciples."

Peter says, "No, no, no, young girl, you're mistaken. No." A second time she says, "No. I saw you. You were with Him." "No, no!" Third time, "You are one of his disciples. Don't deny it." Peter cursed and said, "I don't know Him." And then the Bible says a cock crowed. Peter remembered that Jesus had predicted a cock would crow that night. Peter remembered that Jesus also had predicted that Peter would deny Him three times before that cock crowed. Peter then went away from that fire, ashamed, and he wept bitterly.

Well, look at that. Even those who love Jesus and are very close to Him will at times curse Jesus and run away from Him. But that's not the end of the story. In fact, the only other occasion where a charcoal fire is mentioned is later after the resurrection of Christ, when on the northern shore of the Sea of Galilee, Jesus appears and prepares a charcoal fire. John 21:9 in the English Standard Version reads: "When they got out on land, they saw a charcoal fire in place, with fish laid out on it, and bread." Picture the disciples out on the lake. They don't know Jesus is on the shore. They've been fishing all night and haven't caught a thing, and Jesus shouts from the shore, "Cast your nets on to the other side." They cast their nets on to the other side, pull the nets in, and the nets almost break because one hundred and fifty-three large fish are now trapped and squirming in those nets. It's a miracle.

Peter looks to the shore and he calls out to his fellow disciples, "That's the Messiah." He jumps into the water and he swims to the shore to be with Jesus, who has made breakfast for the disciples. The Bible says when Peter got to the shore, he sat down beside a charcoal fire.

Ears That Are Deaf to the Lies of this World

Consider this very carefully. Why does the Bible repeat the detail about the charcoal fire? Why do we need to know it's a charcoal fire and not a wood fire? What difference does it make? I believe the Scripture is drawing us back to the first charcoal fire where Peter denied Christ. Let me illustrate. When I was a kid, my dad always wore Old Spice fragrance. He doesn't wear it anymore; he's gone on to something better, or at least in my opinion, something better. But, to this day I cannot get into an elevator and smell Old Spice on someone without thinking of my dad. There's something about smells, aromas, and memory.

I think what Jesus was saying to Peter around this charcoal fire was, "Peter, I know you denied me. But don't let that affect you." I say this because He asks Peter, "Peter, do you love me?" Look at the question. "Peter, do you love me?" Can you imagine Peter thinking back to what he did at Caiaphas's courtyard, cursing and denying Christ? He responds, "Yes, Lord, I love you." Jesus says, "Peter, do you really love me?" Peter says, "Yes, Lord, I love you." And then a third time Jesus asks, "Peter, do you agape me? Do you love me like I love you?" Now look at what Peter says in response, "Lord, you know all things. You know that I love You" (John 21:17).

Do you realize that during this whole exchange, Jesus does not correct Peter?

Most of us, if we were in Jesus' position and Peter said, "Listen, Wade, you know I love you." I would say, "Peter, you denied me. You cursed and left me in a dungeon in Caiaphas's house. How can you mean you love me? You're lying." That's what I would say.

Isn't that what you'd say? But Jesus does not! Jesus doesn't correct or rebuke him. When Peter says, "Lord, you know all things. You know I love you." Jesus says, "Okay. Take care of my people."

You may ask, "Wade, what is your point?"

My point is simply this. Rather than your beating yourself up over your mistakes in the past, the God of all grace always brings you to the place where you abandoned Him and says, "Alright. Now get on with it. You're okay with Me. Take care of those around you."

Folks, real redemption recognizes that not everybody lives their lives following after Jesus one hundred percent. But real redemption brings us to the place of realizing we're okay in the eyes of the God of all grace. Now let's go and treat people like He treats us. Are you with me?

So, when somebody calls me, and I know what has happened in their lives because it's been on the front page, how am I to respond? Not according to the way of law. I am to respond in a relational way with grace. I'm to love their pock-marked, scarred life without any expectation of return.

The second thing we see in this text is Jesus saying to the Jews, "If God is your father, you will hear Christ's voice."

I love the story about one of our women church members picking up a young man on the street, seeing him a stranger. It was cold, so she wanted to know if he needed coffee and wanted a ride. That young man has now joined our church. You know, that's a risky move for a woman to pick up a young man on the streets, but she said she felt the Spirit's call. She heard the Savior's voice.

Remember what Jesus said. "The Shepherd goes on ahead of His sheep, and His sheep follow Him because they know His voice. But they will never follow a stranger" (John 10:4).

Now, again, this doesn't mean that there won't be mistakes in one's life as you follow after Jesus. But your Savior loves you. You hear the Savior call, "Cast your nets onto the other side." You hear the Savior ask, "Do you love me?" And you respond. "Lord, You know, I love You, maybe not the best I can, maybe not as I should,

Ears That Are Deaf to the Lies of this World

not as I desire. But You know all things; You know I love You." And the Lord says to you, his sheep, "Okay then, take care of My people."

"My sheep hear My voice, and I know them, and they will follow Me" (John 10:27).

When we were in Israel, one of our ladies was in a parking lot at Bethlehem. We were in the Shepherds Hills, the place where the shepherds were keeping watch over their flocks by night and the Angel of the Lord appeared. We'd just had a devotional and were getting on the bus when our lady found one lamb, one sheep that had wandered away. This was a fairly large parking lot and there were no other sheep within eyesight, save one little lamb who had wandered away. The lady picked this lamb up and held it in her arms. I took a picture and I remember thinking, you know, the Bible tells us that when one of God's lambs, when a child of God begins to wander away, you know what the Shepherd does? He goes after the lamb and in love He catches it and He breaks its leg. This also happens to be the tradition of ancient shepherds.

Now, why would a shepherd break the leg of a lamb? It's because if a lamb is in the habit of moving away from the shepherd, if the lamb begins to run from the voice of the shepherd, the lamb is going to end up being lost. A good shepherd is not going to lose any of his sheep. So, the good shepherd goes after the lost lamb and brings the lamb back, and by breaking its leg he keeps it from wandering away again. Do you know what the lamb has to do until the leg heals? He has to lie next to the chest of the shepherd until healing comes.

Fast forward to today, and the closest modern analogy I can come up with is with our family pet, a new cat. Oh, my word. This cat will climb up on me, stick its nose in my face, come up in my chest, put his ear right on me, and just lie there like a baby. Then I would feel my heart beating and the cat would be moving. That cat was hearing my heart beating.

I thought to myself, when a lost lamb with a broken leg is lying close to the Shepherd's heart, he hears the heartbeat of his Savior. So, I would say this to any man or woman who is committed to following Jesus but has miserably failed in life. God hasn't abandoned you, and we His people will not abandon you. Maybe what God has done is He has "broken your leg" through humiliating shame in order for you to return and hear the heartbeat of your Savior.

By contrast, here's what the scripture says about those who don't know Christ: "But a natural man does not accept the things of the Spirit of God, for they are foolishness to him; he cannot understand them, because they are spiritually discerned" (I Corinthians 2:14).

The natural man, meaning a lost man, does not accept the things of the Spirit of God, for they are foolishness to him. And by the way, the word translated *foolish* is translated *tasteless* in other translations. It's the Greek word *moros*, m-o-r-o-s, from which we get our English word *moronic*. What the Bible is saying is this: the things of Jesus, what Jesus says, who Jesus is, what Jesus has done, all of this seems moronic to people who don't know Jesus. But none of it is moronic to you. That's why you attend corporate worship. God's not through with you. He's not done. The things of Jesus are not foolish to you.

And do you know what happens with people who think that the foolishness of the gospel is tasteless, that it's useless, it's good for nothing? Do you know what happens to churches that miss the gospel and let go of people with pock-marked faces? I'll tell you what happens. They're good for nothing. Jesus said in Matthew 5:13, using the same word *moros*. "When salt loses its potency, its savor, it is moros, it's good for nothing but to be thrown out and trampled on by men." The reason churches are thrown out and trampled down, be-

Ears That Are Deaf to the Lies of this World

coming useless, becoming tasteless, powerless, is because we've lost sight of the message of grace. We're believing the lies of the devil and we've resisted the truth of our Father.

If God is your Father, you grow deaf to the world's lies. Now, it's not that you are deaf, because I really believe deafness is a process. You grow deaf. Physically, the older and more mature you become, the more you grow deaf to the sounds around you. Likewise, the older and more mature you become spiritually, the more you grow deaf to the lies of the world, to the lies of your former father.

So, what are some of the common lies of the world that we want to grow deaf toward?

First Lie: What is most important in my life is "How I Feel." That's a lie. Because the heart of the matter is you may feel miserable, but what is most important in your life is the truth. You may feel miserable because someone who promised to love you has abandoned you. You may feel lonely. But the truth is, He will never leave you nor forsake you, and you will never be alone. What is most important is the truth, not what you feel.

Second. I need it even if I can't afford it. That's a lie. Grow deaf to it. In fact, the Scripture says, "The rich rule over the poor, and the borrower becomes the lender's slave" (Proverbs 22:7). I'm issuing a challenge to everyone reading these words. Stop borrowing. Stop borrowing. And if you think you need it, wait until the Lord supplies it.

Third. If it's legal, then it must be moral. Oh, my word. If it's legal to smoke marijuana, then by all means, I'm going to smoke it. I don't care. It's moral for me because after all, it's allowed by law now. "All things are lawful for me, but not all things are beneficial" (I Corinthians 10:13). The truth that Jesus speaks to your life is far more important than the lies of this world.

The Face of Grace

Here's another one. Fourth. What matters most is my material success. What makes my life matter is my material success. Just look at my peers, look at our neighbors, just look at my brother-in-law. Just look at the things that they own. Man, we've got to be like them. No, you don't. The Word says, "Do not be anxious about what you eat or drink or wear. Seek first Christ's Kingdom, and everything you need will be given to you" (Matthew 6:31-33). Your Lord and Savior says to not be anxious about anything. Don't be anxious about what you're going to eat or drink or what you're going to wear. Seek first Christ's kingdom, and everything you need in this life will be given to you.

So, how do we know that we're people of grace? Well, it doesn't make any difference what somebody else looks like. We're going to move toward them and not away from them, because we love them.

How do we know if we're people of grace? Well, our ears are growing deaf to the lies of the world and we're beginning to understand the truth of our Savior. Truth is more important than what I feel. Truth is more important than what I own. Truth is more important than what people think of me. The truth of my Savior is my meat. It's my food. It's my life. Do you want to be a person of grace? Then I challenge you: Next time you see someone whose life is scarred and pock-marked, why don't you move toward them as Jesus has moved toward you, as Jesus moved toward Peter, as Jesus moves toward every sinner who knows he's in need of mercy? That, my friend, is the *face of grace*.

Chapter Seventeen Discussion Questions

1. When you've done something you really regret, how has it made you think of yourself?
2. What is Jesus' response to our gravest mistakes in life?
3. How can we tune out the devil's lies?
4. As persons of grace, what are ways that we can encourage others who struggle with regret?

Chapter Eighteen

"Ears That Are Sensitive to the Hurts of People"

Ephesians 4:1-2
"…with all humility and gentleness, showing tolerance for one another in love…"

At Emmanuel Enid we're a little bit different. We do not tell people they have to go to church, because we believe that we are the church and wherever we go, God is. When we gather together, it means that we're ready not only to worship the Lord, but to be encouraged. My job is to encourage those who have gathered, and you likewise, also come to be an encouragement to others. That's your job. The people who sit around you are ones you can encourage, so I want to show you how this is done as we continue our study on grace.

What does grace look like? If you have faith in Jesus Christ, the God of all grace has indwelt your heart. The only description we have of Jesus in the New Testament is He was a man full of grace and truth. When we come to know Him, we are called a "little Christ." That's what the word *Christian* means, so that means we're to be persons full of grace.

The picture that you might have of Jesus in your mind is one of a man with long hair, a beard, and Caucasian skin. Recall, that's not the way Jesus would have looked. No, he would have had short hair, he would have been clean shaven and would have had dark skin. He would look more Middle Eastern than the image that you might have of Him from the picture hanging on your wall or in hospitals and other places.

You might ask where we get that long flowing-hair image of Jesus, long well-cropped beard of Jesus with the Caucasian, beautiful smile.

Where does that come from? Well, that's a whole other lesson, but it's fascinating. It's actually an image that the ancient Greeks, the ancient Egyptians and the ancient Romans used as images for their gods, Zeus, Apollo, Isis, and so on. Say, what? Yes, that's true. That's why I would say to you, worship the Lord in spirit and in truth, and realize if you want to know who Jesus is, don't go to a physical image. Go to grace.

Now, what's fascinating about grace is this. We can say we believe in grace. We can teach it. We can preach it. We can sing it. We can even call ourselves people of grace. But are we living lives of grace?

The ancients, when they had plays at theaters would go to what today we would call Broadway. They would go to the theater and watch actors perform. Do you know how acting was done back in the day? They would take a mask, and if they wanted to express happiness, they placed the mask that showed happiness in front of their face and spoke from behind the mask. Or, if they wanted to show sadness, they'd put a mask in front of them and speak from behind the mask of a face that showed sadness. We get our word hypocrite from the Greek *hypokrites*, *hypo* behind, *krites* the mask. A Christian hypocrite is one who presents a public face that says they're a Christian. But in reality, behind the mask, it is false because there is no grace.

I want to remind you what grace is. Grace is undeserved favor. It is a favor bestowed upon someone who doesn't deserve it. I want you to see that a person full of grace will move toward or be

---

Ears that, Are Sensitive to the Hurts of People

Ears That Are Sensitive to the Hurts of People

I'll start off with noting that there is a difference, a big difference between my or your personal hurts, and others' hurts.

We're not talking about slight personal hurts here. We're not talking about you or me being hurt because someone didn't press 'like' on Facebook, or somebody didn't send us a wedding invitation, or somebody overlooked us or didn't speak to us in the hallway of the church. Or maybe when they spoke to us, they spoke in a way that we felt like we didn't deserve. This is not about those kinds of hurts.

Let me ask you a question. Do you often express to other people how hurt you are by the slights of others? If you do, that is the opposite end of grace. A person without grace will constantly talk about how hurt they are from the slights of others, which is the opposite end of grace. For the grace person, they are sensitive to, and move toward others who hurt.

So, let's think about that. How do we know if somebody is hurting? You know, my wife is fond of saying this and it's true, "Hurting people will hurt others." You may have heard it as "hurt people hurt people." The first hurt is an adjective describing people, hurt people. The second hurt is a verb showing action, to hurt people. How do we know if people around us are hurting? What are some of the telltale indications?

Well, first of all they're quick to launch with attacking words, words that cut. They fly off the handle. They are very angry, letting the hurt that's inside of them flare up and outward.

Second, they also assume you're against them. It's merely an assumption, but in their minds they're thinking, "Everybody's against me. The world is against me." Now, why do they assume that? Well, simply put, they can't trust the God of all grace who has the world under His control. They've got to trust their own control. And if things feel out of control, then they assume that you're the enemy because they can't control you.

The third sign of hurting people is that hurt people are unable to see the pain that they inflict on others. The focus is always about the pain that they bear, but they're blind to the pain they give.

Hurt people can't figure out why others don't understand what they're going through. Nobody seems to understand, nobody cares. That's a sign of someone who's hurt. Hurt people are defensive and they never let their guard down. That's why the finger of the hurting person is always pointing at someone else, because the pointing finger says you, you, you're the problem. Saying it or pointing as if to say you're the problem is like a fence with a barb at the end. It keeps people away.

Hurt people don't take responsibility because they're convinced it's everybody else's problem, therefore, it's the others who have to fix it. "It's not me" is their thinking. Hurting people may want to help others, but they never look within to see where the hurt may be within themselves.

Hurt people are quick to react in anger. They're easily offended and because they're easily offended, they'll just come at you with their anger. Hurt people would rather argue than listen, and as a result they rarely have close friendships.

Now, do you know anybody like that? Is there anybody in your life that's hurting? What do you do? The tendency is to move away from them or avoid them, but grace moves toward people who are hurting. It's human to feel grieved when hurting people hurt you, and it's human to want to pull away. But it is divine to move toward that person.

So. Who has grieved you?

Ears That Are Sensitive to the Hurts of People

Guys, listen to me. If you ever want to know what grace looks like in your marriage, it is when your wife who is hurting says things, does things, is quick to anger, makes cutting remarks, but in love and grace you move toward her. How does that strike you? You say, "Whoa, whoa, whoa, whoa! That's impossible."

No, that's not impossible; that's grace.

You know, the opposite of grace is to avoid people. The opposite of grace is to say, "I'm done. I'm washing my hands of this; I'm not going to put up with it anymore."

You might feel justified in saying, "Well, Pastor, I've got to have boundaries."

No, no, you're misunderstanding. Of course, you can have boundaries. We're not talking about that. We're talking about the person who is hurting, the one who hurts others because they're hurting. You move toward them. That's grace.

By the way, this is one of the great requirements for being a pastor. You have to be a person who moves toward people that are offended with you, because if you ever withdraw from people offended with you, you'll disqualify yourself from being a pastor.

Specifically, a gospel pastor speaks good news, and the good news is that the God of all grace moves toward hurting people.

Let's look at Ephesians 4:1, and before we read it, let me set the background.

Any time the Apostle Paul writes a letter, an epistle is what it's called, he'll always begin with doctrine. The first half of the letter will be about what you are to believe, and then he'll make a transition about halfway through his epistle from doctrine to behavior, or your duty based on the doctrine he just taught. Paul never begins by telling you what you're to do. He always starts by showing you what you're to believe. Now, why is it important for us to get the order right? Why must *we believe* correctly before we ever even begin to fulfill the duty?

Why indeed? Well, if you ever start trying to perform before you get your thinking right about God, you will think that it's what you are doing that brings God pleasure. You will think it is by your performance and your achievement that the favor of God will fall on you, because you've earned it by your works. And if you ever start living your life as a Christian by trying to perform in order to please, you've missed grace, because grace comes independent of your accomplishments. Remember that grace is by nature undeserved.

Churches are filled with people who don't live by grace. These church members live by a fundamental code of behavior, a list of rules of do's and don'ts. By nature, they will withdraw from people who don't measure up. They also will avoid people that have slighted them, and in their hurt they will hurt others. This lack of grace is why there's really never any healing.

My mom is a professional editor and she prepared the manuscript for this book. After the first five chapters, she told me that she suddenly realized that what is described here in terms of grace living are the Calvinistic doctrines of grace, just expressed in relational terms. She was very familiar with the theological doctrines of grace, but she didn't recognize them when expressed in terms of relational grace. She said it really helped with her understanding of true grace and what Biblical grace is really all about. Grace is real and recognizable to her now, instead of being just a churchy word that's thrown into sermons and worship songs.

Paul begins Ephesians by telling us who God is and what His grace is like. It's undeserved. "You who were dead in your trespasses and sin, God has made alive" (Ephesians 2:7).

Ears That Are Sensitive to the Hurts of People

You who walked in your former ways like this, like the world, like this and this and this.

But God...! D. Martin Lloyd Jones says the two greatest words in Scripture are the words, "but God."

So, in the first three chapters of Ephesians we saw that we don't deserve a thing from God, but God in His favor toward hurting people has moved toward us.

Now we have Ephesians 4:1, "As a prisoner for the Lord, then, I urge you to live a life *worthy of the calling you have received.*"

He writes as a prisoner for the Lord...what does that mean? A prisoner for the Lord? Well, it simply means God has captured us by His grace. He's taken hold of us. He didn't take hold of us because we deserved it. We were a prisoner in bondage to our sin, but God came, and by His grace He captured us. Now we're a prisoner of the Lord. By the way, I'd rather be a prisoner of the

Lord than a prisoner in Mexico. Been there, done that. As a prisoner in a third-world country, you are trapped in a cramped, filthy cell at the mercy of an unpredictable, possibly inhumane government. As a prisoner of the Lord, you serve Him in your everyday life with joy, secure in His love, protected by His mercy.

Paul writes, "I urge you. I urge you to live a life worthy of the calling you have received." Now, let me pause right there. When I read that verse and come across the English word worthy, here's what I thought to myself, thanks to a fundamentalist, independent, Baptist background. I've got to perform. God's captured me, but now I've got to prove myself worthy. God has saved me by His grace and now I've got to achieve.

That's the way I grew up. By the way, I don't blame my dad for that. He was the son of an alcoholic. He got saved as a teenager out of a family that didn't know the Lord. As a new Christian he was trained under independent, Baptist fundamentalists who said they believed in grace but didn't practice it. And so, as you can imagine it was to some degree transferred to our home. I'm telling you something, I'm so proud of my dad. I have seen the transformation in his life. He was a pastor, but I have seen him transform from a man who once taught grace without living it, to a man who now lives a life of contagious grace and you can't help but catch it.

You see, I used to think that the word *worthy* meant that when God captured me by his grace, then I had to prove myself worthy for Him doing so. No, no, no. I've even heard some people say, "Pastor, listen, I understand that when I became a Christian, all of my sins were forgiven, all my past sins. But now I've got to earn the pleasure of God by what I do now." And I wonder, what are you talking about? Where do you get that?

I can end that kind of thinking by just one simple question. When Jesus Christ died for you, when the grace of God and His undeserved favor was given to you at the cross, was that done only for past sins, or for past and future sins? God sent Christ to die for them all. You didn't deserve anything that God did for you, but He did it. Wow!

In light of this, we are to live a life worthy of our calling. If we aren't meant to "prove our worth", then what are we to do? Well, remember earlier in our study when I covered the Greek word *axios*, from which we get the word *axiom*, a self-evident truth? We applied it to mathematics, when something is so self-evident that we don't even need to compute it, we just see it. Now, let me apply it differently.

Let's go back to Ephesians 4 in verse 1, "As a prisoner for the Lord, then I urge you to live a life *axiomatic* with your calling." You might say, "I still don't understand. How does *axiomatic* relate to *worthy*?"

Perhaps the better word is *consistent*. Consistent with your calling. That's the word *axiom*. In other words, when people see our life, it's an axiom of the grace of God. The grace of God is so self-evident in the way we live, they don't have to formulate what grace is because they see it in our life. This is how we are to live.

The word *urge* in this verse, Ephesians 4:1, means to encourage strongly. It's the picture of a third base coach in T-ball on the sideline, a little kid is rounding third base heading for home plate, and the coach is crying, "Go, go, go, go!" That's what Paul is doing today for us. We who've been captured by the grace of God, Paul is urging to go, go, go. Live your life consistent with your calling.

Paul then goes on in Ephesians 4:2 and writes this. "To be completely humble. Be gentle. Be patient, bearing with one another in love."

I want to zero in on this little phrase, "bearing with one another in love." Because of my personality, which is an Eight on the Enneagram (a system of personality typing), my personality is driven. I have to be careful here sometimes because I am big- picture driven. I'm a visionary. This means I see the big picture and I drive, I drive, I drive to get to the end of the big picture. I'll confess to you that sometimes what happens is I move too rashly. I move too boldly. I move too loudly. I'm not as gentle as God's calling of me is. As a result, I am often seeking forgiveness. I seek my wife's forgiveness all the time. But I know that my life is to be consistent with the calling that God has given me. I am to be gentle. I am to be humble, and not in order to get His favor but in order that you might look at me and see His grace.

Do you remember the Summer Olympics of 1992? Derek Redmond, the runner, was the record holder for the 400-meter dash in Great Britain. He came into the Barcelona Olympics in 1992 as the favorite. He held the fastest time in the preliminary heats in the semifinals. Derek was out in the lead when he heard a "pop" and then he felt pain. At first, he thought he had been shot. He pulled up, and then fell to the ground. He had popped a hamstring. He couldn't run anymore. The world watched as he lay on the track, weeping…then he stood… and began to walk.

Next thing you know, out of the stands ran his father, Jim. He put Derek's arm around his shoulder and held him up, and Derek said, "Dad don't, Dad don't." Jim said to Derek, "Son, we started this together. We're going to finish this together." The crowd then watched Jim Redman bearing up his son, and together they crossed the finish line of the Barcelona Olympics.

That's the word that's used in Ephesians 4:2, "bearing with one another in love."

The same word is used in Colossians 3:13. "Bear with others and forgive whatever grievances you have." Notice the next phrase, "as the Lord forgave you." In other words, you can't bear with or bear up someone else if you've moved away from them. Move toward the hurting; moving toward the hurting is grace.

Now, there will be times when those who are hurting will draw a boundary between them and you and say, "Don't come any closer," or "Stop. I can't." "Get away from me. Don't come." What do you do in that situation?

Well, in respect and love, you stop at that boundary, but you let it be known, "I will respect the boundary that you've created, but I want you to know I'm not moving away. I'm staying right here. And when you're ready, I'll always be here. And when you let me in, I'm coming."

I could tell you story after story, anecdote after anecdote from my own pastoral experience. I say this to our staff all the time, "If we're to be a gospel church and I'm to be a gospel pastor, it doesn't make any difference what people say of me, do to me, how they treat me, I will move toward them. And I will be there. No matter what."

Ears That Are Sensitive to the Hurts of People

I Peter 3:8 reads, "Live in harmony. Be sympathetic. Love as brothers, be compassionate and humble." One way to understand this is that you move toward people who have hurt you.

Now you say, "Pastor, but there are occasions, like in a marriage, where adultery or other things have occurred, and I can't move toward that person because the hurt is too intense and it's too, too difficult." I understand. Just admit to yourself that the reason you can't move toward someone is because you're hurting.

I talk to people all the time, women and men who've been abused in their childhood, and when they hear a message like this, in their minds they're thinking, "I can't move toward the abuser and forgive them. The hurt is way too intense." I understand.

Hold the abuser accountable. They may need to be in jail because what took place is a violation of the law. Absolutely. But move toward that abuser in forgiveness the same way God has moved toward you. If you can't, you can't, but just acknowledge that what may be missing is an understanding of how free and full the forgiveness of God is for you. What may be missing is how unconditional and immeasurable God's favor is for you. So, what I've found is usually this: in our lives when we're unable to be gracious, there's usually a maladjustment in our thinking about the graciousness of God toward us.

To paraphrase what Paul wrote, "I beg you, as a prisoner of God's grace, go, go, go, go, go! Go toward the hurting in grace. And be consistent with the calling that you've received from God."

May God's tremendous, personal, overwhelming grace be something that motivates us in our lives, something that so attracts us to Him that our lives become axiomatic, an axiom of grace in action. May we be those who move toward others rather than those who run from others.

Chapter Eighteen Discussion Questions

1. If you live your Christian life performing in order to please God, what have you misunderstood about God? About grace?
2. When you move toward others that are hurting, what are you risking?
3. When you move toward the hurting, what attributes of grace are you able to show them?
4. How can you respond with grace to a hurting person who rebuffs you, who is unwilling to let you approach them?

Chapter Nineteen

"Ears That Really Hear the Truth of Your Identity"

Philippians 4:11
"I have learned in whatever situation I am to be content."

As we've been looking at the *Face of Grace*, we've seen that I recognize you because of your face and you recognize me because of mine. Our facial features are what help us recognize one another.

Facial recognition technology is exploding. It has become the newest form of security in police work and in places like shopping centers. I wouldn't be a bit surprised if nonprofit organizations like ours use facial recognition technology in the future. Businesses in Detroit have partnered with the Detroit police who are using facial recognition technology. Stores have cameras at their entrance, along with a warning sign saying your face is being monitored and the data is being sent live to the Detroit Police Department. Business has dropped 20 percent in Detroit since that partnership started.

Now, whatever you may think about facial recognition, the one thing we do agree on is this: a person's face is how we recognize them. So, if God is the God of all grace, if Jesus is full of grace and truth, which He is because the Bible tells us that, and if the Spirit of grace resides within us, which it does because as Christians we are each a "little Christ", then we should each be a person of grace and our face should reflect that grace.

We've been exploring what that face of grace looks like. Well, I want to show you that a person of grace has:

Ears that,

Really Hear the Truth of Your Identity

It is the basis of my first book I ever wrote, entitled *Happiness Doesn't Just Happen.*

About twenty years ago I read a book by Jeremiah Burroughs, entitled *The Rare Jewel of Christian Contentment,* and it rocked my world. Jeremiah wrote his book 400 years ago, and I realized that not many Christians today would understand the old English of Jeremiah Burroughs. So, I took the principles of his book, added some color, modified the language, and then wrote my book, giving Jeremiah Burroughs credit for the material.

In his book *The Rare Jewel of Christian Contentment,* Burroughs bases his principles on the verbs that form our text, Philippians 4:11.

Here's that verse in three versions:

- o NAS: "I have learned to be content in whatever circumstances I am."
- o NIV: "I have learned to be content whatever the circumstances."
- KJV: "I have learned, in whatsoever state I am, therewith to be content."

Now I want to show you something about this verse. The word *state* is an old English word for *circumstances.* In the original Greek, the words *state* or *circumstances* do not appear. That's why in many of your translations, they will italicize the word *circumstances* or *state.* The word simply is not present in the original.

Now, the English translators of the Greek did a good job adding it in, because later on in Philippians 4, Paul talks about different circumstances that he's in, or different states that he finds himself in. For example, he's hungry, while at other times he's full. He's in prison and at other times he's free. Sometimes abandoned, at other times with friends. In need financially, at other times, his needs are fully met. Different states and *circumstances*. So, the translators take circumstances as a word and add it back to Philippians 4:11. However it's not there in the original, and Jeremiah Burroughs pointed this out. This is what rocked my world, and here's why.

Look at this verse the way Paul wrote it.

"I have learned to be content in who I am."

Wow!

In this study we're going to ask the question "Who are you?" But before we do, I want to remind you that any text taken out of context is nothing but a pretext. What that means is if you or I ever take a text or verse out of its context, meaning the verses that come before it and after it, we'll end up with nothing but a false conclusion. That's the meaning of the word pretext. So, let's not do that with this verse.

Let me show you the context of Philippians 4:11. Paul's letter to the Christians who live in the City of Philippi was written because he, Paul, needed money. Yeah, that's why he wrote it. And by the way, if you ever attend a church that's embarrassed about asking for money, chances are that this church is probably not doing much. I wonder sometimes if I'm communicating adequately with our church family what Emmanuel Enid is doing globally and locally in terms of missions. It really is extraordinary. But in order to do what we're doing all over the world, it requires money.

Now, I recognize that televangelists and ministries will raise money and tell you they're doing it for this and that and so on, and then they'll go off and splurge on themselves and things that have nothing to do with the original purposes they told you the money was meant for. But that's between them and the Lord. We don't do that. We spend the money we get on exactly what we said we would. Money is a needed tool to do missions globally and locally.

When Paul started out on his missionary journeys, the church at Philippi was one that supported him, then later sent him gifts when he was in Thessalonica. They responded when they knew of his need, and Paul spoke of the incredible joy he has for the generosity of the Christians at Philippi.

When Paul comes to Chapter 4 in this book of joy, Philippians, he speaks of two women in the church, Euodia and Syntyche. I won't burden you with the pronunciation of their names, but my father used to call them Odious and Soon Touchy, two women who really didn't get along.

Here's what Paul essentially says to them, which again you can read it at the beginning of Philippians 4: "Come on, gals. Come on. Be a true follower of Jesus. Where's your joy? In everything give thanks. Stop fighting."

Then it's almost as if Paul kind of checks himself and thinks, "Now, wait a minute. Maybe they're thinking, 'Paul, it's easy for you to say have joy because everything you've asked for has been met. The money you needed, we've given.'" So, Paul, as though he's anticipating their objections, writes (paraphrase), "Oh wait, hang on a minute. When I speak of joy, and you having joy and me having joy (4:10), I'm not speaking in terms of my wants or my needs. In other words, I don't have joy just because you gave me the money I needed. No. I have learned in who I am to be content."

So. Who are you?

Ears That Really Hear the Truth of Your Identity

I'm going to take you back now to an NBA Eastern Conference finals series between the Philadelphia 76ers and the Toronto Raptors. It was Game 7, and Toronto player Kawhi Leonard made a shot with just half a second left. The ball was in the air when the buzzer went off, and it hit the rim, bounced up once, bounced twice, three, four times, and then dropped through the basket. The Raptors won. The crowd erupted. The cameras then turned toward the center for the Philadelphia 76ers, Joel Embiid, and he was bawling like a baby. Twitter went crazy. I mean, this man's a multimillionaire, he has everything a man could ever want, but he's just lost Game Seven and he's crying. Again, no judgment there. It was just remarkable to witness.

I say this because we live in a culture where it seems we are all striving for success, we want to be the best, to be seen as having it all. Winning it all. Being first. Never having a need. Always going out a winner.

Here's that question again. Who are you? Do you realize that when most men answer that question, it's tied one way or another to what we do? I'm Wade Burleson. I'm pastor of Emmanuel Enid, and if Emmanuel church isn't doing very well, Wade Burleson gets depressed, right?

Who are you?

Well, I'm Susie. I'm married to Tom, or I'm the mother of Katie, Jim, and Matt. Most women, and again there are exceptions, but most women obtain their identity and their concept of who they are through the people to whom they're related. By the way, this is completely cultural. Women here in the West take the last name of the man they marry, so is it any wonder ladies get their identity through this relationship. In other countries and civilizations, it doesn't work that way.

But my point is this: Men, when I ask you the question, who are you, you usually think about what you do. That's why when an athlete at the top of his game loses in Game Seven, he's going to bawl like a baby, because he just lost his sense of identity. He's at a loss because he thinks he's a winner, and he just lost. Huh!

You know what I'd love to see? I would love to see somebody be *happy* when they lose Game 7. Full of joy. Content. I'd like a batter to be happy when he strikes out in the ninth inning. You say, "Wade, come on. That's just, that's just not gonna' happen. There's no way any human being can be *content* regardless of their circumstances."

Well, yes there is a way. It's not impossible. Notice that the very next verse in Philippians reads, "I can do all things through Christ who strengthens me" (Philippians 4:13).

You know, I do hear this verse quoted sometimes on television by athletes who are Christians. I mean they're great guys, and they've hit the winning home run. Their team was behind by three runs in the bottom of the ninth with two outs, two strikes. The last batter hits a grand slam and so they win by one. The place erupts, and they go to the World Series and win it too. The reporters ask the person that hits the winning grand slam, "Man, how did you do it?" and the hitter will say, "I can do all things through Christ who strengthens me."

"How did you do it when you made the winning basket, Kawhi Leonard? How did you do that?"

"Oh, I can do all things through Christ who strengthens me."

We all expect to hear this from the winning team, from the hero that throws the last-second jump shot or the receiver that catches the Hail Mary pass in the closing seconds of the game, but it's a jaw-dropper when those words come from one that has "come up short" in the game. And yet it's possible, because it's not the "win" that defines one's "worth."

So, yes, I want to see a batter strike out. I want to see a guy miss the winning basket. I want to see the pastor of a church that isn't doing as well as other churches, see him full of joy. I'd like the reporter to ask, "How in the world do you do it?" and have the person respond, "Well, I've learned to be content in who I am." Have the reporter's jaw drop and say, "That's impossible", and be followed up with the reply, "Oh, no. I can do all things through Christ Who strengthens me."

You see, that's the context we're talking about. Your state or circumstances should not affect your abiding joy as a child of God. Now, often in real life it does, and there's no shame here. If you've been to Emmanuel long enough, you know there's no shame for folks that are depressed and feeling no inner joy because things are going on that just bother them. We're not going to shame you.

What we're saying is,

you're getting your identity from the wrong place.

Your identity, your true identity and your ultimate happiness is found in God's grace and His purpose for your life. So, it doesn't make any difference right now what your circumstances are. What matters is that the grace of God never changes, regardless of your circumstances.

By the grace of God Paul says, "I am who I am by His grace, which is given to me" (I Corinthians 15:10).

All of this now begs the question, who am I by the grace of God?

Well, number one, you're loved. You're not loved because you work hard or because you're a great teacher. You're not loved because you're an excellent pastor. You're not loved because people like to read your books. You're not loved because you're a good businessman that makes a profit. You're not loved because you're a linebacker for the Miami Dolphins and you made the starting team.

No, you are loved because God is love. His love toward you is not a byproduct of your performance. His love is more like an artesian spring, naturally occurring, continually flowing through no effort of your own. It flows even if you "accomplish nothing" and sequester yourself in the same room for the rest of your life. You're not loved or accepted because you do things for this world. You're loved and accepted because the King of Kings and Master of the world has set His affection upon you. That's who you are by His grace.

I'm forgiven. I'm not forgiven just for my past sins. I'm also forgiven today, and for any sins that I'll commit in the future. You say, "Pastor, come on now. You tell people that…and they're going to end up being a worse sinner."

No. No. It's just the opposite. Anytime you're preaching true grace, the logical mind will go to that place of saying, "Hey, I'll just keep on sinning because after all, I can keep receiving God's grace." Paul anticipated that argument in Romans 5 after he talked about grace, and in Romans 6:1 he says, "What? Shall we continue in sin so that God's grace shall increase?"

Me *genoito* (Greek), he says. *God forbid.* That's not going to happen. In fact, it's just the opposite. Do you realize that when you understand what true freedom is, when you understand what true acceptance is, true forgiveness is, it's like a magnet that draws you to the person who loves, accepts, and forgives.

I tell people this all the time in marriage classes. If you're trying to keep your spouse loyal by means of law, you're going to lose your spouse by the law of your dirty look, by the law of keeping a record of wrongs, by the law of your insecure distrust and oppression of your spouse. You're going to lose your spouse.

Ears That Really Hear the Truth of Your Identity

But when you free up your spouse, love your spouse, accept and give grace toward your spouse without conditions, your spouse is drawn toward you. We love God because He first loved us, and we treat others as God treats us. This is the message of grace. This is who you are.

Here's what Paul writes, "And God is able to make all grace abound toward you, so that you, always having sufficiency in everything, may have an abundance of everything you need for every good work" (II Corinthians 9:8). Do you see the word *sufficiency* there? It is the same word that is used in Philippians 4:11 where he says, "I have learned to be self-sufficient in who I am."

The truth of the matter is when we get up in the morning, our first thoughts ought to be on God and His grace for us. We are loved. We are protected. We are guided. We are accepted. We are His. We are justified. We are forgiven. We are adopted. We are blessed.

This is grace, and God is the God of all grace. Jesus is full of grace. God has accomplished for us what we cannot accomplish for ourselves so that in this life we are never called to think we're self-sufficient. Oh, no, no, no. "We aren't sufficient in ourselves to think highly of ourselves. Our sufficiency is of God" (II Corinthians 3:5).

I'm working to disciple a young man who's been broken through some trying circumstances. Previously, this man was proud, cocky and arrogant. And by the way, he also was very smart. But one week into his brokenness, our secretaries let him into my outer office. I was doing a Bible study at 7 a.m. and his appointment was at 8. I didn't know they'd let him in; my inner office door was closed, and I had forgotten that he was coming. For an hour and ten minutes he sat in my outer office, never saying a word, never complaining. He never went to the secretaries, never called me, never texted. Just waited, just waited on me. We had our appointment and it was only afterward that

I learned of how long he'd waited. After he had left without uttering a word about the long delay, I called him.

I said, "Oh, my word. What a change in you." He said, "What do you mean?"

I said, "The old, (and I called him by name) that I knew, never would have waited an hour."

He got choked up and this is what he said. "The old me thought highly of myself. The new me thinks nothing of myself, and highly of God. Why would I not wait?"

Wow!

Learning who we are through the grace of God is life changing. Learning who we are by God's grace is a process of "unlocking the mystery." It doesn't happen automatically, not even close. In fact, where Paul says in Philippians 4:11, "I have learned," learned is a very interesting word. It literally means "I have unlocked the secret" of who I am by the grace of God.

I am an avid reader by nature, and my love of reading began early in life. My favorite teacher in school was the teacher who for one hour would let us read anything we wanted. We would bring our own books to school and we'd put them in a case. If you're a teacher and you're the kind that gives freedom to your kids to read, I promise you will help them in the future. It's one of the reasons I believe I have a mind that thinks visually, because I was encouraged to read when I was young.

When I was a boy, I used to read the Hardy Boys mystery novels. Rachelle knows my personality is such that I've always got to jump to the end of a good book. I want to know. I want to solve it. So, I would read the last chapter, then I'd go back to the beginning and read through the book to unlock all the secrets of the book, even though I already knew how it ended.

Think of your life as a book with God as its author. God has written your book, and He already knows how your life ends. Ephesians Chapter 2, verse 7 says, "For ages to come, God will be unlocking the mystery of His grace to you. He will be showing you the riches of his grace."

Now here's your job. Beginning today, you set aside the belief that you are what you do, and who you're related to, and you start solving the mystery of who you are according to God's grace. I don't care if you've been in prison. I don't care if you've been arrested. I don't care if your name's been on the front page of the paper. I don't care if you struggled with an addiction. It doesn't matter what your secrets might be.

Find out who you are by the grace of God, and you will learn how to be self-sufficient in whatever circumstances you find yourself in.

Chapter Nineteen Discussion Questions

1. What are the truths about "who you are" because of God's grace toward you?
2. Do you presently feel that you're "content in whatever the circumstances", both when things are going well and when times are tough?
3. What's different about a person that exhibits joy in the midst of a defeat?
4. What life experiences have led you to understand God's grace is sufficient for you?

Chapter Twenty

"Ears That Perceive the Fire of God: Grace vs. Judgment"

Matthew 3:11
"He Jesus will baptize us with the Holy Spirit and with fire."

We've spent much time pondering what grace looks like. You and I recognize each other by our faces. If somebody comes up to you and says, "Okay, tell me, how do I recognize grace? What does it look like?" How would you respond? We know that the Bible says in I Peter 5:10 that Jesus Christ is *the God of all grace*. And if He is the God of all grace and a Person full of grace and truth as the verse in John 1:14 says, then we as followers of Jesus Christ, Christians, should be people imitating Him, people full of grace and truth.

In the future, when you think about Jesus Christ, I would challenge you not to think of him visually. We see a picture of Jesus and we automatically think that might be what Jesus looked like, right? There is a drawing that hangs in the British Museum of one of the Egyptian gods of ancient Egypt. The Greeks did the same thing, drawing what they imagined their gods would look like. The Romans followed suit. They wanted images of their gods. And so, they drew them, and they made them Romanesque, long Roman noses, full beards, long flowing hair.

When Constantine became Emperor of Rome and declared the Roman Empire a Christian nation, he had his theologians draw up a picture of what Jesus would have looked like. They basically fell back to the old patterns and drew an image based on the images of their gods. As we covered earlier, Jesus would not have looked like that. He probably would not have had a beard. He would have had very dark skin. His eyes would not have been blue, but brown. He would have been clean shaven, and his hair would have been short. He would have looked like a modern Arab. I know you're asking, "Why the big deal?" Well, here's the thing. When you think of Jesus, I want you to think of him spiritually. He is the God of all grace, and that's what's important to us.

We've got one last verse of scripture we're going to look at as we conclude this series on the Face of Grace. It's just a little phrase from Matthew 3:11. It's the latter portion of that verse where John the Baptist is speaking of Jesus, and he says this: "He (Jesus) will baptize us with the Holy Spirit and with fire."

Now what does that mean? Well, let's look first of all at the word baptize. It's an interesting word because it's a Greek word. In fact, when you read that word in English, you are actually reading Greek. The English translators didn't translate the Greek word at all, they transliterated it. What that means is they took a Greek letter and they put an English letter with it. And so, *baptizo* is the Greek word, while *baptize* is the English word.

But what does it mean? How would you translate *baptize*? It means to immerse. It means to submerge, or, to be totally identified with. The old word was dip. So, when you use the word baptize, you mean to immerse. What this is telling us is that Jesus will immerse you in the Spirit. Who is the Spirit? He's the Spirit of God! But He is called the Spirit of grace. (Hebrews 10:29) And so what John the Baptist is saying to everyone who follows Jesus Christ is, "Listen. Jesus Himself will immerse you in the Spirit of grace." That's how you know you're a Christian.

Ears That Perceive the Fire of God

But it's that last little phrase that I want us to look at. At the end of Matthew 3:11, John the Baptist says, "Jesus will immerse you in the spirit and fire." But what is baptism with fire?

Interestingly, there are three places in Matthew 3 where the word fire is mentioned, in three consecutive verses, verses 10, 11, 12. Let's take a look at these three verses.

First, in verse 10, John the Baptist is again speaking, "The axe is already laid at the root of the trees; therefore, every tree that does not bear good fruit is cut down and thrown into the fire." In this verse, the word *fire* is indicating judgment. It's fascinating that in ancient literature, people were often compared to trees. The Psalmist said the righteous person will be like a tree planted beside rivers of water (Psalm 1:3). Here, John the Baptist is speaking, and he compares a person to a rotten tree. The axe is already at the root, ready to be cut down and cast into fire.

You know what John the Baptist is saying to everyone who's living a rotten life? God Himself is ready to bring you judgment. Now, let's be careful here. It is never our place to judge someone who's evil or rotten. In fact, the Scripture says to take no vengeance on anyone who does evil against us, for as it is written, "It is mine to repay," says the Lord God Himself. "I will avenge." We don't. He does.

So, this is one of the indications we have that Jesus is God Incarnate. That means he is God in human flesh. John the Baptist says, "Look, He's coming, folks. Listen to me. Jesus is coming. I'm not worthy to untie his shoes or to tie the sandals on his feet. But He's the axe ready to cut down every rotten person." Fascinating!

Now there's another verse where the word *fire* is used, and it's in verse 12. Let's skip verse 11 and go to verse 12 where John the Baptist again is speaking of Jesus, "His winnowing fork is in His hand…and He will burn up the chaff with unquenchable fire."

What that means is simply this. If you're a farmer, you know that the winnowing fork was something that you would use to put into your grain that you had harvested. You would then cast it into the air, and the wind would blow away the chaff. The chaff is the husk surrounding the grain and is generally thrown away as useless. Maybe there is a husk that has no grain in it. It's empty. Chaff refers to anything impure. The farmer would use his winnowing fork and throw the grain in the air so the wind would carry away the chaff, then the wheat or barley would fall back to the ground and you'd have your harvest.

What John the Baptist is saying is this. "Here comes Jesus, and He's going to winnow empty people. And he will cast rotten, empty people into the fire of judgment. But that's His job, not yours."

The third place the word *fire* is used is right in the middle of these two verses, in verse 11. It's the same word, but in this second place, Matthew 3:11, fire has got to mean something different than judgment because of the context. "He shall baptize you with the Holy Spirit, *and with fire*" (Matthew 3:11).

He, that is Jesus, shall immerse you. "You" means a follower of Jesus, not a rotten person but a righteous person. Not an empty person but a filled person. He will immerse you with the Holy Spirit and with fire. What is that fire? It's not judgment. Judgment due you has been taken care of at the cross.

What is that fire? Well, that fire is a purifying, cleansing fire. This fire of blessing symbolizes the presence of Yahweh Himself. It's God. He will immerse you, identify you, with Himself.

Who is this God? He is the God of all grace. You say, "Yeah, but you just spoke about judgment." Wait. Judgment comes at the end. Judgment is at the end of the age, and God is in charge of that. He'll separate the rotten, empty people from His people. Let them alone.

Let the wheat grow with the tares, the weeds. These will be winnowed, separated and further, judged. That's His job, not ours. In the meantime, He, Jesus, will baptize you, immerse you in the Spirit of grace and with the fire of God and His grace.

Jesus would refer to this again later. He said, "I have come to send fire upon the earth and how I wish it was already kindled" (Luke 12:49).

Take this verse and compare it to the Great Commission, where Jesus told us to go and share the principles of what He taught to all the nations, "baptizing believers in the name of the Father, the Son, and the Spirit and lo, I am with you unto the end of the age" (Matthew 28:19-20).

What Jesus is saying is this, "I've come to kindle your heart and send you out to be the fire of God's presence to people in need of Him." In other words, you and I ought to

turn every single conversation we have toward grace.

You and I ought to be so immersed in grace that when people meet us, Wow! They experience the presence and grace of God.

This fire into which you are baptized is the cleansing work of the divine Spirit of grace. You remember that on the day of Pentecost, tongues of fire came onto the heads of the followers of Jesus and went into them, for they (and we) are the temple of the living God. (Acts 2:3) When Moses met God at the burning bush, that bush was on fire with God's presence. At the top of Mt. Sinai, that mountain was on fire with God's presence. (Exodus 3:2)

When Jesus was transfigured on the Mount of Transfiguration (Matthew 17), He had the fire of the presence of Yahweh all around

The Face of Grace

Him. When Ezekiel saw the fire of God leave the temple, he saw God's presence leave Jerusalem in 586 B.C. (Ezekiel 11:23) When the shepherds were watching their flocks by night, the fire of God shown all around them, and the angels said, "Unto you, is born this day in the city of David, a Savior who is Christ the King" (Luke 2).

In other words, throughout the Bible, the fire of God's presence is seen. And now here's John the Baptist saying to you, "Your Lord and Savior, Jesus Christ, will immerse you in the Spirit of grace and the fire of God." This is a different kind of fire than the fire of judgment which is coming at the end for rotten and empty people. The fire into which you're immersed as a child of God is the fire of grace that gives life.

Why am I covering this? It's important because this fire of God will transform your environment. Again, you might ask, "How?"

Have you ever felt a dead person? The corpse is cold. When you meet a spiritually dead person, they're cold, but when they meet a person who has been immersed in the spirit of grace and the fire of God's presence, the fire of life oftentimes begins to be kindled within them. That's when you have the opportunity to connect with them, display the face of grace to them, and share the love of Christ. You may be their very first encounter, and you want to be ready.

I want to tell you a story, and I was given permission to tell you by the gentleman of whom it speaks. I was called by the administrator of our local jail, the county jail, who asked for help. He said that they had a very violent prisoner in custody, but they would guarantee my safety if I would come down and visit with him. I said sure I would, and I asked the administrator what was going on. He totld me, well, the prisoner had tried to commit suicide twice by hanging himself in his cell, and they couldn't find a place for him to go. All the mental hospitals, all the behavioral units throughout Oklahoma: Vinita, Fort Supply,

Ears That Perceive the Fire of God

Enid, Oklahoma City, they were all full. Oh, and I'll add by the way, we need more behavioral units. We need more hospitals like that in Oklahoma. He asked, could you see him and do what you can? I said, sure.

He gave me this man's name. The inmate was twenty-six years old and when I Googled him, I discovered some of the things that he had done. He had beaten some people in Garfield County, he had stabbed a man, and was charged with breaking and entering and other crimes in the state of Texas.

So, I went down to the jail and they brought him in. I was expecting the worst, but to my surprise, a broken young man entered in. His eyes were clear. He never looked away from me, but instead looked directly into my eyes. His demeanor was soft. He was shackled, and he sat down across from me.

I called him by name and said, "I know you don't know me. I don't know you, but I'd like to get to know you. I'll spend as much time as you want. We'll talk about why you tried to take your life twice yesterday. But before we do, let's just get to know each other."

He then told me this story.

When he was born, his mom was unmarried, so he carries his mother's maiden name, not his father's name. He said that I probably knew who his father was. He told me his father's name and it turns out that I had in fact heard of him. It seems that when this man was just one year old, his father was put into prison and served a fairly lengthy prison term. He was living with his mother, but then his mother gave him up and he was taken to Enid, where his grandparents raised him from the age of two to about eleven.

A few years ago, his father got out of prison and they were together for the first time at Thanksgiving here in Enid. However, it wasn't long after that that his father committed a horrible crime, brutally murdering a young lady and shooting some police officers, and

The Face of Grace

so he was sentenced to death. I think it may have been in 2014 that the State of Oklahoma executed him, but they botched the execution. You've probably heard of it. The state said the IVs weren't working at the time of execution. His death took 45 minutes, but he didn't die from the drugs. He was in so much torture and pain that he died of a heart attack.

Part of you might be saying, well, his father deserved the death penalty, but the truth of the matter is it was tough. The State of Oklahoma stopped all executions after attempting to execute this young man's father.

I asked him, "Were you there?" He said, "No. I was in prison myself."

You see, this tatted-up young man with a shaved head left Enid and his grandparents at the age of 11 or 12, and went to live with his mom in Dallas. He softly said, "You know, I'm not going to say anything bad about my mom. I love her. I love her to death. She's my mom. But it was hard. It was hard for all of us."

He said, "At the age of 13, I committed a horrible crime." I asked him what it was. I already knew, but I asked him anyway. You know what? He didn't lie to me, he told me the truth and he said, "I received a 10-year sentence. For the first five years, I served it in Juvie in the state of Texas. And when I was 16 years old, I met Jesus."

I said, "Really?" He said, "I did." And you know, I could tell. You can tell whether somebody is genuine when you look in their eyes. He said, "I met Jesus." But he said, "Wade, it has been so hard. They transferred me at the age of 18 to Huntsville, Texas." Folks, I grew up in Texas and I know all about Huntsville. I mean, it's a notorious prison, like Attica in New York. It's a brutal place.

He continued on, "In 2016 when I got out of Huntsville, I didn't know what to do. I didn't know anybody. I didn't know where to go. The State of Texas gives you one hundred dollars. So, I walked out after ten years, from the age of 13 to the age of 23, and I was going to the bus station to buy a ticket because the only thing I knew to do was go back to my gang, because those were the only people that I thought really cared for me. But I heard a horn and my mom, who had moved to Enid to be near her parents, had driven down to Dallas with my younger sister and they had stopped traffic. They had come down for me. They opened the car and they called me by name and said, "Get in the car." So, three years ago I came to Enid.

He said again, "Wade, but it's hard. It's hard. I've done some things in Enid that I'm not proud of." I asked him what he did, and you know what? Once again, he didn't lie to me. He told me what he had done, and I'm telling you what, it was gruesome. That's why the jail administrator told me he's probably going to get a very long sentence in prison in Oklahoma.

But I listened to this young man tell his stories. He was handcuffed, dressed in his prison jumpsuit. And he said this, "I need to be in cuffs. I need to be here because I'm doing what I don't want to do, and I don't know why I'm doing it." I said, "Well, why are you trying to kill yourself?" He looked at me and said, "Wade, I'd rather be in heaven than to continue the way I am and keep straying from God."

Obviously, I've compressed this story. Let me tell you what I did after that. I leaned in close. I called him by name and said, "Listen to me. I know we've only known each other for a brief time. But I want you to know I love you and I believe in you as a person. And God loves you. I want to ask you a question. Did Jesus come to die for good people or for rotten people? For empty people?"

He said, "For rotten, empty people like me."

I said, "Yes. Listen to this verse: This is a faithful saying and worthy of your full acceptance, Christ came to die for sinners" (I Timothy 1:15).

I continued, "But let me make this personal. This is a faithful saying and worthy of your (calling him by name) full acceptance. Christ came to die for a man who (and then I went down his rap sheet). God doesn't die for people He doesn't believe in."

He began to weep. He said, "So you're saying God doesn't want me to take my life?" I said, "No. God's got a purpose for you." He said, "What's that purpose? I may be going to prison for decades!"

I said, "Do you know how much we want to be in McAlester Penitentiary to tell people the good news of Jesus Christ, and we can't be there? If you're in McAlester, do you think guys are going to listen to you? Look at you. Look at what you've done. Listen to who your dad is. Do you not think that guys who are there because of their crimes are going to listen to you? Maybe. Maybe God, in His love and belief and faith and grace for you has a purpose for you that you don't even yet comprehend. But I'll tell you this, if you begin to comprehend it, Emmanuel Enid, my church will commission you to share the good news in McAlester."

You could just see his face begin to lighten up. You could see, you could see life coming into his eyes. You could see him warming up. You know what I was doing? What I was doing was giving him grace. All I was doing was showing him faith and belief, the fire of God.

We talked some more. I answered his questions about Jesus and about the spiritual attacks from the enemy and so on. But when it was all over and done and I prayed with him, he said, "Wade, if anybody says there's not a God, they're wrong. God is right here."

I said, "That's exactly right."

He said, "By the way, did you say your church is Emmanuel Enid?"

I answered, "Yeah." He said, "That's my church." I nearly exclaimed, "What?"

He said, "Oh, yeah. My grandparents, they're members of that church. The best years of my life were when my grandparents would take me to Emmanuel from the age of when I can remember, 2 to 3 years old until I was 11. I went to the children's events. The first, the only Christmas that I ever had with my family, then it was my mom and my dad, it was Thanksgiving and we went to that little building that your church owns, the Grace Place. I remember being there and my dad was there for the first time. And then every Christmas we'd come to this show and there was this guy that would do the books of the Bible at the end. I loved it."

I said, "That was me!" He looked at me and he said, "That was you?"

He gave me permission to share his story. And I share it because I want you to know that if I'd gone to the jail that day and I'd judged him and shamed him for everything that he had done, if I had seen a broken man who came in wanting to take his own life, and I self-righteously gave him the law, I would have left there and he would have remained cold. But when you see somebody broken, it's your immersion in the Spirit and the fire of God's grace that will bring life.

This fire of grace, this fire of God's grace not only gives life, this immersion in the Spirit also creates longing.

When somebody is in the presence of God's grace, they want to know more about this God.

Listen to what the prophet Isaiah said: "The Lord's fire is in Zion." That's another way for speaking of Calvary, Mount Zion, "His furnace in Jerusalem" (Isaiah 31:9).

If you want to know about the glory of God's grace, you find it in the face of Jesus Christ, who gave His life outside the gates of Jerusalem on Mt. Zion.

Oh, and this fire of God also kindles love.

The Face of Grace

When a man becomes warm to the God of all grace, when he begins to understand that God has a gracious purpose for his life and then all of a sudden, he's captivated by the love of God, what's he going to do? He's going to love people who need love. Love, which the world regards as a weakness becomes the basis of all goodness and is the productive soil in which everything good grows.

This whole series is designed basically to say that Jesus has immersed you in the Spirit of grace, and the fire of God's presence. Now, go give life to rotten, wounded, empty people. People that are broken over their rottenness, their wounds, and their emptiness. Watch how the fire of God's grace changes them now, so that the fire of God's judgment won't consume them later.

You might say, "But Pastor, now wait a minute. Your argument may be right, but come on now, there's got to be law somewhere. All this talk about grace is just cheap. There's a lot of people out there that aren't broken. There's a lot of proud, arrogant people, and they need the law. Surely they've got to pay somehow." Yeah, you're right. I agree.

But you know, I find it absolutely stunning that the church seemingly gets this in reverse. We go out to a world that's not broken, a world that's proud and arrogant and shaking its fist at God, and we tell them God loves you and has a purpose for your life. And then when they give their lives to Christ, we bring them into the church and feed them law, law, more law. It ought to be just the opposite. The law is used to break people. But when a person is broken, you don't ever give them law. You give them grace.

We were driving back from Oklahoma City recently. We were on Highway 81 in a construction zone where the speed limit goes down to 45 miles an hour. And then in one section it's 35 mph going north to Enid. Honestly, I never want to be behind anyone when we get into construction. I want to be at the front so I'm the one going through first, right? Well, I'm trying to get by a guy on the highway. The speed limit's like 65, I think. And so, I was going 70 because you can go five miles over, not get a ticket and so on, so that I could pass him on the left.

Well, he wouldn't let me pass. He speeds up. I'm like, what is this guy doing? And so what do you do? You've either got to pull back or do what? Speed up! So, I went faster. Guess what he did? He went faster. I mean, it's crazy now. My wife is saying (remember she's of a different personality), "Wade, stop. Just pull back." I won't tell you how fast it got. But he would not let me go. So, I finally pulled back and I called 911. Yes, I sure did. Got them on the phone and told them who I was. I said, "Listen, this guy's driving recklessly. I was just trying to pass him. He wouldn't let me pass." They asked my location, I told them and said, "I'll be right behind him."

So, down the road at Kingfisher, three law enforcement officers: the sheriff's department, the local police department, the highway patrol, all pull in right behind and pull him over. I stop too, get out and walk up to their car. Four juveniles get out of the car. My heart begins to soften at the sight. They get out and they're standing there, so I walk over and I ask, "Officers, can I speak to these young men?" They said, "Absolutely." So, I stood in front of them. I said, "Guys, what were you doing? I was just trying to pass you on the left. You wouldn't let me pass." The guy driving said, "I don't know, sir. I don't know. I'm sorry."

One of the officers then says, "There's drugs. There's drugs," and they pull out the drugs. The guy who was driving is high. You could just see him begin to melt. My heart softened even more. I said, "Guys, you're in trouble. I want you to know I do hope it works out for you." I'm sure they'll know who I am.

I got back in the car. The police officers came over and they thanked us. They said, "You know, we can't be everywhere at once. And thank you for calling us in." I said, "You know, officer, I typically would never do that, except for the fact that they were very aggressive. We were coming into a construction zone and he wouldn't let me go by." He said, "No, no, no. You did the right thing."

But here's my point. Sometimes the law is needed to break people of their pride. But if you ever meet a broken person, don't give them law. Let them feel the fire of God's grace. May we all understand that God is the God of all grace. We've been immersed in the Spirit of Grace. Let's do our job of taking grace to broken, empty, rotten people and let God and His law deal with people who are unbroken. May it ever be so.

Chapter Twenty Discussion Questions

1. From this point on, how ought we picture, or think of Jesus when our thoughts turn toward Him?
2. Jesus says, "I've come to kindle your heart and send you out to be the fire of God's presence to people in need of Him." Which kind of fire is He referring to?
3. What effect should that fire have on those we have been sent out to?
4. When is it necessary to apply the law? When is grace necessary?

Final Challenge

Prayerfully consider this: If you looked into the mirror of God's grace, how much of His Face would you see? What facial features are evident, and which ones ought to become better defined? Ask the God of all grace to so captivate your heart, that you too will reflect

    the Face of Grace

www.ingramcontent.com/pod-product-compliance
Lightning Source LLC
Chambersburg PA
CBHW050314120526
44592CB00014B/1899